PRAISE FOR

Conversations with Grace

"A blueprint for your soul, mind and body. Julianne Haycox brilliantly weaves her own adversity with Divine light and optimism. *Conversations with Grace* lends inspirational hope and reaches pathways within ourselves to heal and transform. Her insight into nature teaches there is more to just a walkabout. A true must read I couldn't put down!"

—**MARY K. SAVARESE**, author of *Tigers Love Bubble Baths & Obsession Perfume (who knew!)*

"Haycox shares gratitude and grace for the trials and tribulations in life. Her own personal journey is both mystical and divine, providing an inspirational and well-written read."

—**ANGELA CORRELL**, author of the May Hollow Trilogy

"*Conversations with Grace* is the best heart-centered metaphysical book I have read in years! It is pure wisdom from the within to the without, written by a heart that already knows."

—**REV. DIANE ROACH**, esoteric healer and spiritual counselor, author of *The Vital Art of Not Knowing*

"Julianne's masterpiece, *Conversations with Grace*, is an inspiring and compelling memoir that will leave you feeling armed with the tools to redefine life's challenges as gifts meant to get us back in sync with our inner self, our sense of purpose. A lesson in perseverance, faith, hope, and love. Read it, share it, gift it!"

—SIXTUS Z. ATABONG, PA-C DFAAPA, author of
My Father's Gift: How One Man's Purpose Became a Journey of Hope and Healing

"*Conversations with Grace* is an inspiring and inspired personal memoir. Julianne Haycox provides an intimate, spellbinding and authentic look at her life; she always finds the good in every situation and has a gift for reframing challenges through a positive lens. Through her memories and vivid descriptions, Haycox shows readers the true meaning of *grace*."

—KATHLEEN REID, author of *Sunrise in Florence*

"I was privileged to read the human document, sharing a journey of transformation from inquiry, through courage and determination, to a place of peace and joy. I particularly appreciate Julianne's affirmation of the efficacy of prayer and the spiritual oneness of all living things. Her most wonderful gift is the gift of self!"

—DR. WILLIAM C. HEDRICK, Tidewater Pastoral Counseling

"Julianne Haycox has created a treasure chest of spiritual and natural wisdom in this small volume. Dealing with tremendous loss at midlife . . . Julianne chose to change the conversation with herself and others. Deciding that 'grief is not a place to stay,' she embraced Native American wisdom and a mantra of silence through which she heard the sound of healing and discovered the power of mindful words to change our lives and the lives of others. In *Conversations with Grace* Julianne uses her beautiful and powerful prose to offer her readers the opportunity to journey with her as she goes 'straight through the fire to get to my soul.'"

—SUSAN CUSHMAN, author of *Friends of the Library, Cherry Bomb, and Tangles and Plaques: A Mother and Daughter Face Alzheimer's*

"One will call this a book, but in truth what Julianne has created here is an incredible collection of experiences accompanied by the very thing that matters most to us all, inspiration and the beautiful ability to see these experiences from a space of love. We felt her pain, we celebrated her joyous moments, and we were reminded that we are all one! Get your highlighter; many of Julianne's quotes will make your heart sing and soul breathe easy!"

—BRENDA AND GUY HOFFMAN, *The Pixie and the Bull*

Conversations with Grace

by Julianne Haycox

© Copyright 2020 Julianne Haycox

ISBN 978-1-64663-003-5

Published by

◤ köehlerbooks™

210 60th Street
Virginia Beach, VA 23451
800−435−4811
www.koehlerbooks.com

Peace & Blessings to you

& Julianne

CONVERSATIONS

with

grace

JULIANNE HAYCOX

VIRGINIA BEACH
CAPE CHARLES

I dedicate this book to everyone in my life; past, present and future.
Thank you for the love and the lessons.

AUTHOR'S NOTE

I do not aspire to share with you my expertise; I have no such thing. I do, however, have life experiences that have afforded me the gift to navigate my challenges while learning, growing and evolving. I feel with all my heart that these lessons are meant to be shared and to bring comfort, faith and a true sense that a healing love exists within everyone.

I have likely not remembered every event in this book exactly as others present might remember. Perceptions and memories differ from person to person. My words come straight from my memory and straight from my heart.

INTRODUCTION

An Awakening

WE GO, GO, GO—chasing after the day, the night and the "list." The lists are all around us.

They are stuck to our planners, refrigerators, dashboards, phones and computers. They are everywhere. These lists take up prime, front-row space in our daily lives and keep us working into the night. Keep working out at the gym more than the next person. Keep buying everything that the "it girl" is obsessing over. Keep doing what everyone else is doing and what others want us to do so we don't miss out. The words *YOU ARE MISSING OUT* should be stamped in bold, black ink across every list out there!

I realized that I was missing out when my life took a sharp turn. The stamp came down like a gavel upon every list, every well-sorted plan and everything I thought I needed. It became clear that it was time for me to face my fears and my truths. It was also time to walk out on the life I was living and leave some relationships behind me. I took my heart with its hairline fracture and burst it wide open so I could get closer to my soul. I had no choice but to let go and find my way back to myself. This process was crucial to my happiness. And it was intentionally guided by every painful event that became my lesson. This arduous assignment came at a very specific time in my life. I knew that this mid-course correction was my only choice. My mom had just passed away on the twenty-ninth of December 2014, and ringing in the new year, my fifty-third, would be solemn and veracious.

The first fifty years of my life were not free of hardships. I've certainly endured my share of life's lessons. But it wasn't until the death of my mother and watching as a friendship of twenty-five years slipped away that I felt a monumental shift in my hibernating core. I suddenly stood parentless and as the one not invited to the party. There were nights that tears of fear and confusion dampened my pillow and many days when the tears gently washed my cheeks and dried in the midday sun. The despondency would show up unannounced and whenever it pleased. The pain that temporarily resided in the pit of my stomach became a part of me and took over as it scraped out what existed inside of me and held it up before my eyes to view at close range.

The cycle was initiated in July 2013 when I was faced with the unsorted reality of friendships that were ending. The time was lonely and comforting. It was scary and encouraging. It was numbing and intense. It was difficult but uncomplicated. As time unraveled, my reality became clear. This was another section torn from the manual of my life. I knew that I needed to examine my course and allow the innate wisdom to show through in black and white. I knew that this shift was worth more than any second thoughts.

I was in my early fifties sitting on the sidelines of my own story. The bleachers were empty. I was the sole spectator. I was ready to observe and scrutinize who I really was. Sitting in my silence, without distractions, was where I would have the best view of my reality. I knew that this would take courage and tenacity. I also knew that it wouldn't all be pretty.

Luckily, I am very comfortable being alone and quiet; I just hadn't honored this passion of mine in many, many years. Ever since I was a little girl, I cherished being outdoors. When I think back to my very early teens, I see a curious little girl content playing all by herself in the quiet beauty of a forest filled with pine trees. Fifty years later, that love was rekindled with the peace, growth and forgiveness of nature's cradling ease. Once again my heart filled with the miraculous beauty in every leaf, in every petal and in every wave. And once again I felt the captivating comfort in the kindness and awareness of a bird's song. All of this patiently and graciously waited for my renewed attention.

I was finally returning to what I've always loved and found solace in. This kingdom of awakening is where I uncovered the truths about myself. Nature moved me and moved with me. In the quiet and solitude I met with my thoughts. It was in these thoughts that I realized how grief and pain were taking up sacred space in my life. I wanted to fill my sacred space with sacred thoughts. There is so much beauty to experience and so much peace to embrace in nature. Out in this magnificent realm, my thoughts became free from the grip of judgment and fear.

What sometimes felt like isolation and loneliness soon became a blessing as the natural world revealed extraordinary gifts simultaneously with the very thoughts that were crossing my mind. In the winter months of 2015, while sorting out the death of my mom, I began writing in a journal again, something I had faithfully done as a young girl. Radiant joy from the gifts of the natural world began to fill my soul and the empty pages of this new life of mine that was ready to unfold and expand. I was in the embrace of God and Universe. I felt it. I saw firsthand, and I was in such awe that I wrote every experience down to remind myself of the miracles that show up when I show up.

In the silence and solitude, I would ask, "What else could this mean?" I wanted to see beyond my habitual thoughts. Initially, the answer was muddled and dull. I needed more time, more stillness and more space to begin to understand and clear my way to the truth.

The aspects of my life most needing my attention blazed through my uncomfortable memory like a laser beam. There was no need to summon the recollections, and I could not push them back; they arose on their own with clarity and intention.

Bumping up against my past relationships, my losses and my previous behavior gave me the opportunity to choose whether or not I would hold them as hostile prisoners in my gut and heart or set them free with grace. I chose to change the conversation with myself and with others. Freedom and grace felt better. I chose conversations with grace.

CHAPTER 1

Love Is Stronger Than Death

MY FUTURE APPEARED TO be erased with one phone call. My oldest brother, Paul, the one person that I turned to all of my thirty-three years of life for sage advice and unconditional love and respect, had had an accident. Paul was the oldest of the seven children in our family. The high regard that my parents held for his first-born status lasted throughout his forty-five years of life. He could do no wrong. I, on the other hand, was the last-born child in the family and was fondly referred to by my mom as "the mistake."

There were twelve years between my brother and me, but the gap closed over the years as the two of us became incredibly close. In my adult life I leaned on him more than ever. Complicated relationships surfaced in my life, and he guided me through them. When we talked on the phone, I felt his presence as if we were sitting right next to each other. The best gift he gave to that little girl years ago and continued to bestow upon me was his willingness to listen deeply. He quietly listened to every word, and he listened to the pause. As I think back on our conversations, I realize that it was in this pause that we connected.

He gave thought, deep thought, to who I was and what I needed. I have never experienced anyone so completely present. He spoke to me from his heart, with a gentle and clear regard for my well-being. He was never harsh, yet always honest and true. I had never experienced such ease and freedom to be myself as I did in his presence. It was as if he knew what was missing in me and he had a way of guiding me toward that. He was another set of eyes, consciously observing my life with understanding and wisdom.

I moved from Michigan to Virginia after my high school graduation. I was seventeen years old and searching for a bigger life than the one that I was living in Michigan. I will never forget the morning that I left. My dad was sobbing and my mom had a glorious smile on her face as she held out a bag of sandwiches that she made for my journey. I had purchased a 1966 Volkswagen bug with my hard-earned $660, and I boldly kickstarted it the entire way from Michigan to Virginia where I lived for a while with my brother John and his wife and baby. The bond with my brother John developed in Virginia. He became my protector. I felt his protection and love, and I was proud of what we shared. I enrolled myself in Old Dominion University and quickly found a job and started my new life. Although I left my family behind, my brother Paul and I were always just a phone call away from each other. We talked a lot. He had a beautiful way of letting me figure out the solutions to my problems as he listened and gave me the space and love that I needed to clear my head.

His heart was so big and so true and so constant. I felt like a thread of love and understanding connected us through our lives, and this bond warmed my heart. But on this freezing-cold and dreary day in February 1995, my heart stopped. I truly felt the thread pulling away. I was so scared, and the onslaught of fear pushed my mind into overdrive.

"There has been an accident. Paul is in a coma. I'm just not sure what will happen," his wife, Vicki, gently said over the phone. I knew that she dreaded having to say these words as much as I dreaded hearing them.

Vicki's words launched like a torpedo and propelled straight through my heart. The burning surge burst into my gut and thrust through my throat, stealing my breath and my words. Tears swelled in my eyes. A sudden, deafening pressure felt like a steel rod being driven into my ears, and I felt as if my skull would rupture. My chin and lips trembled imagining Paul's kind face. It was as if someone else were controlling my body. Searing heat filled my nose. An uncontrollable sobbing broke loose. Everything was numb and excruciatingly piercing all at the same time. There was no containing the harrowing pain. I closed my eyes, trying to relieve the intense throbbing. I felt so, so sick. My legs relinquished their support of my shaking body. I couldn't feel my arms. I wanted to drop the phone. I had heard these words before. I never thought that I would hear them again. Wasn't once enough?

Paul's first accident was in 1968, when he was eighteen and I was six years old. When he jumped from our garage roof into our swimming pool on that hot summer night, life as all of us knew it changed forever. I awoke to the loud sound of sirens and ran to the window to see flashing lights fill the darkness in our backyard. There was so much panic on everyone's faces. My parents were horribly shaken and then they were gone. The ambulance carrying my brother was gone. The flashing lights were gone. All of a sudden it was painfully quiet and dark. I went upstairs to our cedar closet. This was my safe place, my refuge.

My mom spent all of her time at the hospital. For Mom, under normal circumstances it was a full-time job to keep our family of nine together and moving forward. In that time of our lives, her perseverance was tested. She was up against a wall. I saw it in her tired eyes and heard it in her occasional sharp tongue. But she was strong and unwavering in the face of this life-changing impasse. As a mother, she was grateful my brother was still alive. And she focused on keeping our ship afloat.

My dad digested his new life very differently than my mom. It was best to be on your finest behavior or hide when dad returned home from the hospital after work.

Before Paul's accident, my dad and Paul shared the same ambitions and plans for my brother's life: Paul would play hockey in college and go on to play for the Detroit Red Wings. This game plan was always in clear sight. My brother was a great hockey player. Dad was fully invested in Paul and the game of hockey. Dad coached my brother's teams when he could and never missed a game, ever.

After Paul's accident, Dad (like Mom) was also grateful that his firstborn child was still alive, but his dreams for his son were dead. With one seemingly harmless jump from our garage roof into our backyard pool, my brother edited his life and forced my dad to trade his dreams in for a life he had never given thought to.

I had just turned six years old, so my view of this new life was muddled with confusion. No one ever sat down and explained things to me. Any knowledge that I had came from picking up what a six-year-old could from an adult conversation, and a very brief and edited version of where my brother and the rest of my family now spent all of their time.

Strangely, one of my clearest memories from this time was fearfully unpacking my lunch at school. My seventy-year-old grandmother stayed with us while my mom was away at the hospital all day. My grandmother was an amazing baker. She made the best cinnamon rolls! I longed for those hot, delicious cinnamon rolls, but lunch was not her strength. After day two of opening my lunch bag to a ketchup-soaked white bread bologna sandwich in wax paper, I quickly closed my paper bag to the horror inside and made do with the apple that was thankfully unscathed by the red slop. I couldn't wait for Mom to come home to us and properly pack our lunches again. Everything felt different at our house. It was painfully quiet during the day after school and on the weekends while everyone was at the hospital, but then, when they came home, a different pain filled the room.

Finally, the wonderful day came when they brought my brother back home. Paul was now almost nineteen years old; he had spent his eighteenth birthday in the hospital. I was seven years old, soon to be eight. I was so excited to celebrate our August birthdays at home, together! Prior to his arrival, changes were made in our house to accommodate his new life. A hospital bed now commanded the space of our den. When I watched as the bed was brought into our house, I felt so happy that my big brother was coming home. I carefully placed my small, wooden rocking chair next to his bed. I was so excited to have a friend to sit with. I couldn't wait to see him.

They wheeled him up and into the back door on a wooden ramp that my dad carefully constructed by hand. The tables in our house would now be too low for my brother when he sat in his wheelchair, so dad made a tall table that was the perfect height for my brother. When I think back to that time, I remember the thick plastic mug filled with ice water and adorned with a straw that always sat on the table. Paul would hook his arm around the mug and gently pull it just close enough so he could lean into the straw and have a sip of water. A Velcro brace holding a fork that fit on his hand and gave him the freedom to feed himself also sat on the table. For Paul, these minor details represented independence.

Prior to and upon his arrival home, my parents seemed nervous. I suspect that they wanted to be sure that everything was just right and in place so the transition into his new life would be as comfortable as possible. My mom's only nursing education came from her unexpected two-year residency at the hospital as she helped care for her suddenly paralyzed son. The nurses and doctors gave her almost everything that she needed to provide my brother with the best possible at-home care. She taught my older sisters a few things to occasionally lighten her load. I, on the other hand, was blissfully unaware of the exhausting daily routine required to ensure that Paul got out of his bed, was showered, shaved and immaculately dressed. My brother had always been meticulous about his personal grooming and his dress, and my mom granted him this one small thing in his life where so much had been taken away from him.

Mom was determined to make it all work. Her resilience was amazing. I am beholden to her for respecting and granting the few things that she could to maintain my brother's dignity and sense of self. And I am forever grateful for the years that I spent in my little wooden rocking chair talking the days and nights away with my brother, who gave me his undivided attention and taught me so much.

When Paul moved out of the house in 1975 to attend Michigan State University, he continued to include me in his life. I was a very loved and proud teenager riding on the back of his electric wheelchair all over the huge campus during my visits with him. We shared long conversations about life. We went out to dinner together, just the two of us. He was bigger than life to me.

Twenty-seven years later, my brother lay in the hospital again. This time I was an adult, so I was fully aware of what was happening. I learned that, this time, he wouldn't be coming home. I immediately packed my bags and got on the next plane to Detroit. The plane ride and my mind were a thick, foggy blur. My thoughts were held hostage by confusion and fright. On the hour-long drive from the airport out to the hospital in his rural neighborhood, the grim reality ahead ticked closer and closer as the miles passed behind me.

Before this wave came crashing in, my brother was fine. In fact, his life was exploding with good things. He and Vicki were just days away from finalizing the adoption of a little boy. Paul loved his job as a drug and alcohol counselor, he cared deeply for his patients, and his patients loved him. He adored his wife and his family. He loved life and he took nothing for granted. I loved and admired everything about him, and I was so proud and thrilled for him and Vicki and the amazing love and life they had created together.

Throughout Paul's adulthood, he was incredibly independent and self-sufficient. He drove a fully equipped handicap van and got around in his electric wheelchair quite well. On the day of his second accident, he and his dog, Stanley, were on a walk in the woods of his backyard when Paul leaned forward as he had done hundreds of times for this very task: to empty his leg bag. But this time, his arm missed its hook on the handle of the wheelchair, which had always served as his anchor. Without the secure clutch on the handle to hold his body upright, his upper body uncontrollably slumped forward. He, being a quadriplegic, could not lift his body back up to a sitting position. Stanley barked and barked, but by the time Paul's neighbor found him, over ten minutes later, he was unconscious. At the hospital, the doctors determined that Paul had gone too long without oxygen and the damage was irreparable. Paul remained on life support until his dear wife, Vicki, made the dreaded decision.

I was so grateful to be with him when he passed and so grateful that Vicki gave all of us ample time to get to his side. Our last goodbye was never spoken, but I know that he was still listening. I know that he will continue to hear me because it was he who taught me how to listen. He had a smile on his face when he passed. The room took on a very ethereal energy, and I could feel his presence behind me, supporting me as he always had.

Grief is not a place to stay. As painful as it is, why would we choose to stay? Yet, some of us set anchor and let it wash over everything that should be celebrated.

When my brother died, I stayed in the grief. I was stuck in the mud of my fear—fear of life without his sound, compassionate, empowering guidance. He was a master at bringing me to the answer that waited within me. Little did I know he was preparing me to look inward and nurture and trust my own awareness. He was preparing me to live without him. His existence was a salve, and when he passed, I had to learn to live without it. I was rebellious to the thought of living without him. I wanted to miss him. Missing him made me feel closer to him. I wanted to scream out that no one else in this entire world could replace him! I wanted to cry out to the Heavens above and convince God that he was mistaken. He took my brother too soon.

Time didn't dilute my longing to see Paul again. I tried everything to ease the pain and distract my attention from the gaping loss. I needed to find a place to feel love in my heart and dissipate the grief. So, I dug up and replanted my entire yard.

Having my hands in the dirt was therapeutic, and washing the mud and dirt from my face down to my feet at the end of a hot day felt like washing away a bit of the sediment of my grief. I drove for hours in my car listening to Paul's favorite songs at full volume so I could cry it all out without bringing anyone else in my family down. During my curative three-hour drives down the interstates between Virginia Beach and Richmond, I purged emotions and felt every pain that I could pull out from deep inside. I cranked the music up so loud I felt the throbbing bass cracking my chest open and darting through my body. The music pushed the pain through me. I felt alive and I felt Paul's presence, as if he were perched on the sun-roof laughing at how loud the music was playing. I sang his favorite songs at the top of my lungs, knowing that he could hear me.

I felt free and crazy good singing my way out of the cage of grief. Singing felt so much better than the guttural cries that had been stealing my breath and my joy. The soulful drives were a welcome and healing release. When I stepped out of my car and into my home, I was lighter and stronger; inspirited by love, I knew that I was not lost. I hung on the words of Robert Plant's "Little by Little." I made a little bit of progress in releasing the clinging grief. *What is next?* I thought. And then one day a friend asked me if I had ever tried painting.

I purchased an easel, canvases and acrylic paints and brushes and set everything up, including my hopes for a way out of the deep grief, and I painted. My first painting was very dark with a hint of gold light. After my husband's encouraging and kind approval of my first painting, I wanted to continue. It felt good to paint. I felt like my emotions were right there before me on the canvas, so I could see them clearly. I saw a flicker of light in this hold of darkness. After a few days, I carried myself back upstairs to my easel to paint again.

This time, I chose much lighter colors, earth tones and white with a dab of red. I mixed some of the colors and brushed the canvas with the paint. Something just didn't feel right; I felt disconnected. I put the brush down, dipped my hands into the paint, and my arms and hands, as if orchestrated by something other than me, began to move smoothly and harmoniously, accelerating across the canvas. About twenty minutes later, my arms and hands stopped and dropped to my sides. I was exhausted and standing before the most beautiful angel I had ever seen. I am forever grateful for this experience that funneled straight from Heaven into my heart, dispelling the pain and darkness and filling me with hope and light and the power of faith.

There was a palpable, glorious shift in me that day. The power to move forward arose in me. I felt my brother's love surround me. My heart was nestled in a safe place of understanding. I held the warmth in my heart and preserved the beautiful vision of his kind face. I will always carry his gentle voice in my most treasured thoughts, knowing that his sage advice is just a quiet moment away.

Now, Paul is my guiding spirit, one of many. The pain has developed and refined me, helping me to grow into and trust myself. Death is discovery—discovering your strength in overcoming sorrow; discovering that the gift your loved one left you is real and will always exist within your heart and soul. Remembering the lessons that you learned from them and the life you shared together is how you bring them forward with you and keep them alive.

I have experienced many deaths and learned so much from each one. Life continues to rearrange. People move in and out of our lives, always leaving something behind. Maybe something we have learned, something we have loved, or something we must learn to live without. Each relationship, each bond, each hurt is a seed planted within us for the growth of our souls. And one day, beautiful petals unfold and reach for the sunlight, having grown from fertile soil, tilled with life's compost and nurtured with time, patience, love and care. And so, the circle continues with every changing season of our lives, nourishing our souls with love, strengthening our faith with lessons, and ultimately bringing us to wholeness and peace. I now feel resolve and truth resonating in these words of Rumi: "Goodbyes are only for those who love with their eyes because for those who love with their soul there is no such thing as separation."

CHAPTER 2

Paul Phillip

WE HAVE A CHOICE when adversity drops in to our lives. We have a choice on how we will see it and how we ultimately respond. When I was presented with what some might consider a kiss of death, I saw something else. I turned away from the darkness that tried to coax me into the murk of anguish. I would not surrender to obscurity. I looked for the light. I reached for it inside of me and fought to keep it burning, stoking the fire with faith and the spirit of an eight-year-old girl who taught me to trust my own strength.

I witnessed remarkable courage and calm in a sweet little girl named Jasmine, who chose to give all she had to each day, in spite of facing a terminal illness. I will never forget her beauty and virtue, and I will forever hold her love and wisdom in my heart. I was thirty-one years old, living in the third year of wedded bliss, and I had just sold my business. I was happy to leave behind the twelve-hour workdays and excited to fill my free time with something meaningful. The Children's Hospital of The King's Daughters in Norfolk, Virginia, was always close to my heart and a simple twenty-five-minute drive from my home. Jasmine became my hero and my lesson as I watched her valiantly fight cancer.

Despite her illness, her dark-brown eyes sparkled and her little mouth was like the petals of a rose, unfolding into a glowing smile, greeting each new day and every visitor. The moment I walked into her room and laid eyes on her beauty through pain, I swallowed my fear and any and all heavyheartedness. There just wasn't any space for hopelessness in her room; it was already filled with every machine you could imagine and, most importantly, a little girl who chose to focus on the simple beauty in every day she had.

I'll never forget the first time that I mentioned to the team of nurses my idea of taking Jasmine outside for a walk. It was a beautiful, warm, sunny day—the perfect escape from her dim, sterile room beeping with the constant reminder of her illness. Her head nurse, Kate, wanted to squash the idea; I could see it on her face. And then, Kate's inner hero came through.

"Let's do this!" Kate said.

I felt her power and determination, and with my excitement, we walked into the room and told Jaz the good news. Her sheer delight extinguished the piercing *ding, ding, ding* of machines monitoring vitals, and Jaz's spirit of hope sent us through the roof!

If only for a walk, this escape would be executed in style. Kate pulled a beautiful, white eyelet dress from the tiny closet—one of several heartfelt garage sale purchases these angelic nurses made for their beautiful Jaz. The dressing process was long and surely painful due to the requisite maneuvering of the cords that pushed medicine into Jasmine's veins to fight the cancer, boost her immune system and stifle her pain. Jasmine gracefully fought back each stabbing pain; every uncontrollable jolt was quickly eclipsed by her solid reassurance to continue. I savored the thought of Jasmine feeling the warm sunshine and fresh air on her face as her beautiful white dress billowed in the breeze. She radiated pure love and dignity amidst it all. I found myself wondering, *How does this happen at the tender age of eight?*

I was thirty-three when I was called to fight my illness. In November 1995, I was diagnosed with cervical cancer. The diagnosis wasn't the fatal blow: I was beginning the second trimester of my first pregnancy. The reality of it all thrust straight through my heart. Everything happened so fast.

Just one week before the dreaded diagnosis, we saw our baby on the ultrasound, with the heart beating beautifully and strongly. And then the phone call came from my doctor. I called my husband, Rick, at work as I fought back the pain. He came home with fear in his eyes and tenderness in his touch. We drove to the doctor's office in a thick silence.

On the drive home from the doctor's office, the silence was searing. My heart was broken, and glancing at Rick's swollen eyes, I knew his was broken too. Once we were home, the blistering silence was doused with phone calls and concerned loved ones ringing doorbells. I wasn't sure if answering all of the questions and repeating the painful information over and over again overwhelmed my husband or if it helped him to slowly process everything. I craved silence and connection, and Rick was kind enough to afford me this little bit of time with my baby. The quiet and stillness was where I could make my connection. I wanted to say how sorry I was that this was happening, and as I sat with the guilt, a still, small voice graced my thoughts: "We're going to be ok; we will always be together." As gentle as a feather falling from above, I felt a pure sense of oneness with my baby that changed my meaning of forever.

The next morning, I was in the hospital having a radical hysterectomy. I was given consistent prognoses by the team of doctors that suddenly assembled around me; there was no escaping the truth. The pregnancy was accelerating the growth of the cancer. I was told that neither my baby nor I would make it to full term if I chose to continue with the pregnancy. My baby, if it made it, would not have a mother: I simply would not survive at the rate the cancer was growing. I couldn't believe that this was happening.

The veil came off of the feelings I'd had all along. From the beginning of my pregnancy I felt deep down inside that I would never hold my baby in my arms. The occasional spotting that I experienced was a quiet confirmation of my intuition. My pregnancy, even before I received my cancer diagnosis, never felt right to me. It never felt real. It never felt tangible. The cramps and the light bleeding would bring tears to my eyes that I made sure no one else saw. I didn't share this fear of losing the baby with my husband; he was so innocently hopeful. I didn't share this with anyone. I hoped that my intuition was wrong and I would never have to speak my fears. The same feeling that was telling me that I would never hold my baby also kept me hanging on to discover the meaning of it all. I felt that there was something else, something that looked like hope just around the corner, but in that moment I stood in the harsh face of loss.

I felt my life being disassembled and rearranged, and I made a choice. I would let the reconstruction evolve. I trusted. I felt tucked in and safe despite the cancer and the extraordinary loss of my baby. I felt the work of the Divine at play; I felt it all around me, enveloping my body and holding me. This innate presence bolstered my strength and intrinsic faith. The spirit of promise embraced me. These inspiriting words of Rumi fell into my lap just when I needed to absorb the essence of hope in the message: "Stay with it. The wound is the place where the Light enters you."

I knew the Divine was supporting me through this horrific experience because of the role that timing played in all of it: Paul, my older brother who I adored with all my heart, died in March of 1995. I found out that I was finally pregnant on my thirty-third birthday in August—just five months later.

Getting pregnant was not easy. My husband and I had already been patients of the Jones Institute of Virginia for over a year. Drs. Howard and Georgeanna Jones were a gift to so many parents struggling to have children. They were pioneers of hope, giving our country its very first in-vitro fertilization baby.

And with the many successful pregnancies that the institute had, I was filled with promise. I decided to take a pregnancy test on my birthday. When I saw the positive test, warmth melted over me. I felt my brother's presence with a gentle intensity—this was my birthday gift from him. I could see his face and his kind, knowing smile in my mind's eye.

Walking through the doors of the quiet hospital at 6:00 AM the morning after receiving the worst news imaginable was a solid affirmation of the loss and emptiness that would soon take over and silence my insides. The walls seemed to close in as I walked through the hallways.

The hospital, a small Catholic one, was the only option for the emergency surgery that I would undergo. The waiting room was filled with family and friends. They had all been blindsided just like me. I felt their fear. Everything was moving too fast, and because of this, there wasn't time for quiet conversations. There wasn't time for any conversations at all. The air was clogged with the discomfort of unfounded expressions of hope. No one knew what to say. Tears were all they had. I was relieved to be taken from the waiting room to my pre-op bed.

While I waited to be wheeled from the small pre-op room to the operating room, sadness tried to elbow its way into my heart. And just as I felt myself giving in to the darkness, a modest but inspirited nun walked into my room and allowed the light back in. I suddenly felt a familiar comfort in the sanctity of this hospital, dropping in from my earliest memories of my Catholic upbringing. The nun brought a much needed tenderness and sense of peace into the sterile room. When she asked if I would like my baby baptized, my heart filled with hope and my eyes swelled with tears.

This sacred tradition meant so much to me in that difficult moment. It was what I had left to give my sweet baby. All I could give was this blessing and all of my love with all of my heart forever and ever. If our baby was a boy, he would be baptized Paul Phillip after my brother Paul and after Phil, my best friend from high school who was killed in a car accident a year after we graduated. I will never forget opening my mailbox and taking out a handwritten letter from Phil on the very same day that he died. His funeral was on my birthday. Our friendship was special and everlasting. If our baby was a girl, she would be baptized Christine, after my sweet grandmother who had passed on just two years earlier than my brother. After waking from a six-and-a-half-hour surgery, I was told that our baby was a boy. He was blessed and baptized Paul Phillip.

The first night in the hospital was rough. I fought off the stabbing pain in my abdomen with a continuous dose of morphine. In the dark of the night, amidst a layer of fog that blanketed any coherent thoughts from my mind, the night nurse fumbled and nervously admitted she had almost given me the wrong medication. Her inexperience didn't afford her the ability to gloss over her mistake. She looked so young. *Is this her first shift?* I wondered. I was just relieved that she caught herself before she shot my veins with who knows what. Despite her mistake, I didn't feel threatened at all. She had learned a valuable lesson: we were in this together.

After that experience, I felt very awake, yet confused from the drugs and very alone in the dark room. My stomach hurt so badly along the deep incision. I wished I hadn't sent my husband home. I needed him. I wanted to hold his hand. I called home after the nurse left the room. My husband insisted on coming back to the hospital. It would be a thirty-minute drive in the middle of the night. I convinced him that I would fall back to sleep soon after I hung up the phone, and

I did. Just hearing his voice was comforting.

The next morning I awoke to Paul's wife, Vicki, standing at the foot of my bed. Vicki was a registered nurse and the most quietly compassionate person I knew at that time in my life. She had flown in from Michigan to Virginia to be by my side. When I saw her, the fear and loneliness left the room, and my heart swelled with love. She sat with me through the pain. She did everything an experienced tenderhearted nurse could do. She did everything a big sister could do if her baby sister were in pain. She stayed. She slept in a chair for three of the seven nights that I was in the hospital. We didn't talk a lot. We didn't need to. I felt safe with her there. I felt my brother's presence so strongly.

The very next day brought another angel into my room: my love-filled and dear friend Martha. She was truly an angel on earth. Martha is tall, but not so much in the physical sense; she is elevated in a sublime sense. Her hair is golden, long and tousled perfectly. Her blue eyes are a sultry sea of love and compassion, drawing you into her faithful focus. She came in and filled my room with a luminous, radiant energy that manifested hope and love. Her husband, Larry, who was battling the final stages of his cancer, was too weak to come up to my room.

Larry was also extraordinary. His wide smile was a little bit crazy, crazy enough to draw you in closer, where his love took over. His salt-and-pepper hair and beard and his tan, slender face beaming with clear-blue generous eyes usually gave me visions of him in a white robe and sandals. He was a noble man with the ability to illuminate beautiful emotions in others. These two amazing friends graciously set aside their pain to ease mine. The true love they shared with one another and with me warmed my soul in a way that I will never forget.

Larry was another kind of savior. In my mind's eye, I could see the tender smile upon his face as his frail body rested in the front seat of their car. I felt his ray of love shine through my window from the hospital parking lot. The world was a better place with him in it.

Just two months later, the earth shed tears as he passed on. Those that truly love him continue to feel the vibration of his innately exuberant spirit through the silence of his voice.

I was overwhelmed with the love that surrounded me with every visit, through all of the beautiful flowers and gifts and from the true friends who always showed up. Each connection strengthened me.

After one week in the hospital it was time for me to go home. My body did not feel ready. It hadn't kept pace with my mind, which was so eager to seek meaning and renewal. I had not eaten solid food in over a week. I had lost twenty pounds. My physical body felt weak. My abdomen was swollen and swarming with discomfort, but my insides seemed to lie dormant. I was unable to pee because of the swelling, so I went home with a catheter that stayed with me for one month. Long skirts became my uniform and concealed the temporary setback.

During the radical hysterectomy, my insides were scraped and most of my lymph nodes were removed from my left side. My left leg and foot soon revealed the distress through swelling. I found a lymphatic drainage–massage therapist who soon became my saving grace, dear friend and confidant. I got used to wearing the compression stocking and looked forward to my treatments and warm conversations with my newfound friend, Linda. Linda came to my home to give me my treatments since I couldn't yet drive and she believed that the treatment should begin right away. Our sectional lounging sofa in our den provided plenty of space for me to stretch out my swollen left leg and foot while leaving ample room for Linda to sit and work her magic on my depleted lymph system. My abdomen was still swollen and very tender to the touch, but I trusted her expertise and her loving intention, especially around the site of my incision—the very place where life crashed into death and horror posed hope. Linda was twenty years older than me. She came to me with the compassion of a loving mother and the complete presence of a best friend. Her sparkling blue eyes held both tenderness and humor. She was a breath of fresh air.

Just getting out of bed and moving to another area of the house where life was taking place was healing in itself. My sweet husband had everything organized along the kitchen counter—a bed tray, coffee and tea cups, napkins and utensils, all ready to serve up a little love and care. As I walked past the kitchen, I could feel myself there soon, creating my own concoctions of nourishing food. This small goal brought solace to my intention of healing in my own time and on my own terms.

I had already spent a long and grievous week in the hospital bed that seemed to engulf and hold prisoner my battered body. And though our bedroom at home was filled with natural light, unlike the dark hospital room, I felt an uncomfortable connection between the two beds where my burning loss lingered in the silent darkness of sleepless nights.

The doctors insisted that I needed a lot of rest. I knew this, and my body begged for it through sheer exhaustion, but my mind continued to swirl around the what-ifs, what was, and the whys.

Resting on the sofa in the mornings was my reprieve. The wall of windows faced east, and the warm light of the morning sun scattered a welcome and restorative embrace. I have always loved the early mornings; everything feels new and unscathed, and possibilities feel fresh and available. I would sit thinking and wondering what might be next. I listened to the still, small voice inside of me and stared for hours at the great blue heron in the cove, sending me His message to be still and know.

In my mind these were all just temporary disruptions. These hardships had a meaning, a lesson and a gift. I was sure of this. God never wastes a hurt, and I knew these challenges wouldn't last forever.

I gave privilege to the lessons—the ones I had already experienced and the many still on their way. Trust was the catalyst of my healing, and honesty was the process I needed.

This is why when the doctors wanted to buffer my mending with antidepressants and more pain pills, I refused. They tried to convince me that I needed these meds because of the hysterectomy-induced hormone imbalance and the loss of my baby. Instead, it was my baby's beautiful face that gave me strength, and it was his essence that would heal me. I promised myself to stand noble and steady in his honor. It was through this integrity that the blessings came. I was able to clearly understand and absorb their worth.

Returning home from the hospital was almost as wrenching as leaving for the hospital on that dreaded morning. It didn't feel like home anymore; instead it felt as hollow as the inside of my body. The air felt stiff and pale. An uncomfortable quiet slunk about. Even my sweet dogs, Yogi and Baloo, were unusually doleful. As time moved on, the air became clearer. It became easier to breathe. The night sweats stopped—the morphine was out of my system. The physical pain was subsiding, and my thoughts awakened. The words of this poem came to me with the sunrise one day and brought needed warmth to my soul.

My tiny baby boy sent here to give me life
and a voice for hope.

Welding a place in my heart to be held by you and only you.
Your beautiful, soft face so vivid
in my thoughts and visions that grace my days.

Your skin is olive; you're so healthy and strong with full black
hair and dark, glossy eyes twinkling with love.

It is through your eyes that we connect.
It is as if there is a river rushing beyond the beautiful spheres
of tenderness.
The water is rich with wisdom and divinity.
Together, we float over the blueprint of my life.
Your vision is clear.
The fog of what is yet to come blurs mine.

That first night home, my husband tucked me into our bed with everything I would need within my reach. His sensitivity was the warmest blanket of all.

My loyal canine companion Yogi kept watch over me, tucked up close on the floor next to our bed. He had always slept on the bed—at the foot for the previous ten years. We didn't forbid him from getting on the bed upon my arrival home from the hospital—Yogi just knew. He and I were as connected as two souls could be. Our relationship and his instinctive understanding brought such a profound comfort to me at that moment in my life.

The next morning was Thanksgiving. I knew I had so much to be thankful for, but the morning brought a spell of sadness that fought to tether itself to my heart. As I prepared to stave it off, our dear friend Lonnie walked into our bedroom with a pumpkin pie that he had made himself. Tears of relief and gratitude for this rescue filled my eyes and ran down my cheeks. Once again love prevailed. During the challenges and the pain, everything counts. And not only does everything count—everything is magnified. Acts of love and kindness settled into my heart, burrowing in so deeply they became a piece of my grateful soul forever.

That pumpkin pie would be the extent of our Thanksgiving that year. In the past, the holiday was a blur of cooking, cleaning and preparing to host my family for a feast. Over the years, we hosted family that lived in Virginia and sometimes family from Michigan and New York. But my parents always stayed with me and Rick since our home served as the perfect midway point in their winter migration from Michigan to sunny Florida. In previous years, it had been important to me that they were comfortable, entertained, and fed their favorite foods. I was always exhausted after their one-week stay with us, but in the year of my surgery I was too exhausted to even consider hosting a visit or a holiday. I wanted to heal my body and my mind with honesty and purity. Time and space were what I needed to feel and recognize my true emotions. I would not succumb to a temporary fix or hurriedly brush uncomfortable feelings under the rug. I wanted to face this head-on and stay true to the experience and the lesson.

Disease and illness can feel like a ghost—a dark shadow without a face that creates fear and illusion. But the ghost can only exist if we allow it in. Instead of allowing my illness to use me and become its vessel for despair, I used my illness as a source of wisdom. I scrutinized every layer. I questioned: Where was the disease in my body? At what time in my life did it show up? How healthy was my lifestyle, my habits and my thoughts? How healthy were my current relationships? What about my past relationships? I knew that every aspect of my life was interconnected. What messages were asking for my attention?

Acceptance of the lessons allowed all of the fear to fall away from me. I knew that I was not going to die. I held this conviction with all of my strength. I held on to it through the struggle and the wavering beliefs of others. I felt unshakable knowing that I was supported by a Divine source. My will to live and learn was commanding. The adversity, pain and loss led me to understand and know myself on a very different level. My spiritual growth opened up as I changed my perception and let go of fear. The wounds became a resting place of discovery, trust and love.

Since my parents had missed sharing Thanksgiving with us, I didn't want them to miss out on our Christmas together. Christmas was a festive feast, and they looked forward to it. I'll never forget my dad walking in from a quick grocery store run that he had made for me. His hands were full and his arms extended toward me with a red poinsettia arrangement adorned with red taper candles. Red was not my favorite color and poinsettias were the only flower on this earth that I had an aversion to. But, on that day, I saw right past my distaste and into my father's tear-filled, apologetic eyes.

He cried as he told me how sorry he was that he and my mom never even called or sent a card to me while I was in the hospital fighting my cancer and mourning the loss of our baby. His regret was so raw. He didn't know that I had already forgiven them, so I held on tight to that floral arrangement and gave him a hug. Everything would be okay. After all, I was the last of their seven children, and I had spent most of my life tending to and fending for myself. This time in my life was not different. I never really gave it much thought with the exception of quieting my husband's storm of disbelief over my parents' apathetic behavior. There was no sense in holding them accountable for behavior that might be expected or standard. I didn't have room for that in my life or in my heart. Instead, I cherished the intense closeness that I felt with my baby boy each and every day.

I felt him all around me, and in every vision he was smiling. His smile brought me love and taught me love. This love was so supreme that I couldn't think of tarnishing it with resentment. Besides, I had formed a close bond with my "chosen" family, made up of my husband, his incredibly compassionate and funny mother, and several close friends and family. People that chose to be with me surrounded me with an abundance of love. I felt the amazing presence of God, angels and Paul Phillip in my very soul, and that was all that mattered.

CHAPTER 3

Austin Rae

TRYING AGAIN IS THE secret. I do believe that God leads us by the desires of our hearts. My ovaries were saved and I had all the faith in the world that we could have another baby. What I endured with my illness and what lies inside of me, and before me waiting to unfold, is mine to bring to light. The desire and faith was luminous in my heart, and I knew my intentions were within reach. I fed my faith, and not the fear or doubt that occasionally floated into my thoughts. It was time to gather all of my strength and move forward. The only reason to look back would be to honor my baby boy, to reach for his hand and bring him along on this magical journey that he granted me by saving my life.

In August 1996, just nine months after my radical hysterectomy, Rick and I met our surrogate mother, Gwen, along with her candid and very easygoing family in Sacramento, California. In 1996 surrogacy was a bit of a mystery, especially in Virginia. As much as we had read and researched, we sought the comfort of the most accomplished hands within this delicate field.

The morning of our flight out to the West Coast was somewhat typical of a travel day, with the obvious exception of my whirling excitement. I checked through all of the last-minute details and was ready to give Yogi and Baloo their "going on a trip" hugs and treats when a pain struck my lower abdomen so hard that it brought me to my knees. My breath was taken away. My face flushed with heat. I had never felt anything like this before, not even after my recent surgery. This was something new, something full of power and something that wanted my attention. Minutes later, it was gone for the most part. I still felt exhausted. I stood up slowly, feeling like the wind had been knocked out of me. My heart pounded with joy for the inspirited blessing. Once again, a higher power had made an entrance into my life, and I knew it.

Later that day, at the surrogacy center in California, Rick and I sat talking with the doctor. I mentioned to him that I had a very strong feeling that I was at the beginning of my cycle and running some blood work might be a good idea. The doctor suggested that my earlier abdominal pains could have been from nerves. I knew otherwise, and he was kind enough to support my intuition. I realized how complex this whole process would be, and every little bit of blessed favor was not only welcomed, but honored. He ordered an ultrasound and blood work.

Later in the afternoon, after meeting with the doctors, we met Gwen for the first time. I was so excited! We felt an instant closeness. It was comfortable and effortless. There were no awkward spaces to fill with small talk; we fell right into each other. I told her about the incredible cramps I had that morning before leaving home in Virginia, and I shared my hunch that I was at the beginning of my cycle.

The next morning, she excitedly called to tell me that she had just started her period. I've never been so delighted about a period in my life! My hopes were sky high. When we arrived at the fertility center the doctor told us that the ultrasound showed that I had already ovulated and the blood work confirmed that I was also at the beginning of my cycle. The doctors were amazed that our cycles were perfectly aligned. They had never seen this happen without manipulation. This was a confirmation to me that I was exactly where I needed to be. I had made the intended connection.

With our cycles perfectly in sync, we were able to move forward immediately. There would be no time spent finding my cycle and taking medicine to align mine with Gwen's. Had I not been attuned and opened to my soul and the Divine at work, who knows how long the road would have been and where it would have taken us. Trusting my intuitions and listening to the gentle voice inside of me allowed so many blessings in. Feeling and experiencing God and Universe communicate directly with me elevated my life to a place of expansive harmony that I never want to forsake.

Three months later, in November 1996, our embryos were transferred into our surrogate. Ten days after the transfer we received the amazing news that the implant was successful—we were pregnant on our very first try! This year, Thanksgiving brought even more for us to be grateful for, and this year, we celebrated. The next nine months were magical. Rick and I wanted to be as much a part of this pregnancy as possible. We flew out to Sacramento for each and every doctor visit, and I was Gwen's coach during our birthing classes.

Our high-resolution ultrasound at twenty weeks, our halfway point, was a memorable appointment. I was full of butterflies and excitement to see our baby on this remarkably clear and vivid ultrasound. Gwen, on the other hand, was solely focused on the huge jug of water that she was instructed to drink before the test—all without using the bathroom. She wasn't feeling quite as light on her feet as me! She showed up with two huge jugs of water—one for her and one for me. I proudly drank all of the water and held it in right alongside her. I would do most anything that Gwen asked of me, and I would do so with the same esteem that she always showed me. Drinking the jug of water didn't faze me; nothing could bring me down from the cloud I was floating on in anticipation of seeing our baby. The sooner we could make the water disappear, the sooner our sweet baby would appear on the screen!

Over the ten months, Gwen and I became so close. We spent a lot of time together. Neither one of us held back: we were both willing and open. I was older than she by several years. Our trust in each other created an intimacy and an incomparable bond. She would ask for advice, and in answering I was as discerning as I would be with my own daughter or close friend. I truly cared about her and loved her.

We were brought together by this miraculous undertaking, but our focus wasn't always the pregnancy. She had a life despite her benevolent commitment. Together she and her husband, Bruce, had four children. Their personalities were distinctive. Each of the kids was welcoming, warm and fun. Their enthusiastic interest and support of us was another blessing. We shared family dinners with non-stop boisterous conversation swirling around the table as the kids let their voices ring loud and clear. The pre-teen sense of humor on display was entertaining and invigorating. The girls loved to sing for us while we relaxed outside in the warm California evenings after dinner. Each one of us was openhearted and engaged in these new friendships. Each one of us had something to give and something to receive.

Our due date was another undeniable omen: August 2 was Paul's birthday, and we were having a girl! The ten months went by quickly for all of us. As the due date came closer, we were already missing each other and the comforts of the relationships we had built. Even now, as I reprocess the day that our baby girl was born with all of its wonderful synchronicity, I find it hard to recreate the ultimate masterpiece that it was with simple words on paper.

Although the baby's original due date was Paul's birthday of August 2, our little one decided to enter the world on my grandmother's birthday, July 24. My grandmother and Paul were incredibly close.

They had lived very close to one another, and the connection they shared was sweet and strong. My sweet little Czechoslovakian grandmother passed away just two years before my brother.

I wanted to stay there—in this place where God and Universe were reaching out and leading me forward. Drop by drop, blessing by blessing, my heart filled with light and love. I was sure that the entire floor of the hospital in Sacramento was filled with this energy of love and accomplishment. I felt that this energy radiated into every room and surrounded every soul. This love could not be contained. My gratitude for the wonder about to arise was infinite. My tribute to God and Universe for this miracle circulated through me and vibrated through every cell of my body.

There were nine of us gathered in our surprisingly spacious birthing room at the California hospital: Gwen and her family, me and Rick, and a dear and supportive friend from Virginia along with her husband. I was grateful the California hospital rules were more relaxed and conducive to a private and personal experience. Those that wanted to stay in the room through the birth were welcome to stay. Everyone stayed.

I wore one of Paul's polo shirts; it brought me strength and comfort. I can still feel Gwen squeezing my hand until I lost feeling in it. I had no idea the intense pain she was feeling, but I wanted to take it away from her. All of our laughter and playful times over the past ten months were swept away as the reality of the pain and sacrifice of giving birth blew in. I wanted to hold her and stop what looked and sounded like sheer agony.

And then I came to my senses. I was her coach! I was not here to crumble; I was here to be her rock, her guide back to the ever-important breath, her comfort, her encourager and her hand to squeeze the feeling out of.

Suddenly, there she was. Our sweet little girl was on her way out! And through the fog of excitement, mental exertion and pseudo-pushing, I heard the doctor ask who would be cutting the cord. I stepped in as we had discussed. I could barely see what I was doing through the tears. When I made the cut, blood sprinkled across my brother's pure-white shirt. I looked down for a split second as if directed, and I felt my brother's presence. I glanced over at my husband standing on the opposite side of the bed. His eyes were filled with tears—he looked so vulnerable and joyful. The strength of our marriage has been weaved together by festive milestones and happy times, but the adversities weaved the thickest, most solid fibers of our existence and our bond. I felt so much love for him.

The room was bright with love and tears of faith and joy. I am forever grateful to every single person in the birthing room that day. Each one brought an extraordinary gentleness and burrowed a shining space forever in my heart.

Austin Rae, our beautiful baby girl, came to us like a soothing balm, mending the wound in our hearts and replenishing our spirits. While looking into her knowing eyes as she rested snugly in my arms, I felt a wringing out of the somber emotions; the sadness and grief of the loss of our baby boy changed into hope and a deep, deep love for both of our children.

I'll never forget how I felt that day in the California hospital. I can instantly recall the magical symphony of events. A subliminal and unspoken promise slipped into my heart that day—a promise to live and share every beautiful blessing.

I felt the shift within myself, inspiring me to live by example for the lives that I have been blessed with. This was an exercise in decency and self-improvement as I simultaneously began to shape Austin's life. When I looked down into her innocent face and at her tiny brand-new body swaddled in my arms, I felt an earnest sense of responsibility to stay a course of truth, authenticity, temperance, strength and compassion. After all, I would have a tremendous influence on this brand-new life, and I wanted to cultivate a virtuous being. I inherently wanted to honor God and all that had a hand in her life by bringing forth a girl who would be self-motivated, independent, kind and authentic, and most importantly a girl at peace with herself so she would creatively, courageously and lovingly help to make this world a better place.

It seems a blink away since Gwen and her husband, Bruce, came to our home in Virginia to celebrate Austin's first birthday and live for a few days in the life of the little girl she helped bring into this world.

Austin's birthday party was filled with all of the traditions. Gwen was quite an accomplished cake baker, so together we baked and laughed as Gwen taught me how to decorate two three-dimensional bear birthday cakes. One cake was for the guests to eat and the other for the birthday girl to dig her hands into! It was a joyous and simply perfect celebration.

The years following Austin's first overflowed with fun, laughter and lots of love. Our little girl loved to dress up—every single day. Layering was her thing. Skirts over dresses, tutus over skirts, necklaces upon necklaces, hats, sunglasses and dress-up shoes with fancy socks—and shoes that didn't always match. She loved to read books out loud to our dogs, her infant and toddler cousins, her grandparents, or anyone that would listen, which often meant her stuffed animals, her dolls and her imaginary friend. She loved to dance and sing, and she loved to talk. She loved to make forts in her room and all over the house. She loved to paint and bake and eat raw fish—she loved life, and we loved our parts in this larger-than-life world we shared.

As she got older; middle school age, she loved school, her teachers, and most of all, her friends. These friendships spanned from pre-school through high school and straight through to today. Our house bustled with screaming girls for years. They started with sleepovers, at-home dress-up performances and lots of parties. And through middle school and high school the girls all played sports together, got dressed for proms together, spent summers at the beach and on the water together, and they laughed and cried together.

In 2016 we celebrated Austin's admission into college. She's not a little girl anymore. Her dreams are big and her aim is high. She had her mind firmly set on one university. I felt the joy of the solid opportunities she had. She felt the seduction of uncertainty. I will never forget the moment that she hit the button on her computer to reveal the email that arrived as scheduled. I stood in the doorway of her bedroom and watched her sink into relief as her tears flowed. The valve of fulfillment was opened, releasing all of the fear and doubt as the coveted acceptance to her favorite university finally came. Thank God for all of it. I've told her time and time again that God has a plan for her just as he does for all of us.

During her biggest disappointment in high school, that statement was what I told her, and I believed it with all my heart. I told her that this desire-turned-disappointment was not part of the plan for her life, and as I sat next to her on her bed while she cried and doubted herself, I felt her open up ever so cautiously and let faith in. What I saw next in her made me smile. She listened to her inner voice, envisioned her horizon, dug up her passion and persisted toward it.

In the spring of her tenth-grade year, she traveled to a small village in China with Operation Smile, an amazing organization that repairs cleft lips and palates in the most underserved places around the world. She came home with photographs of the beautiful children and the doctors and nurses that changed her life. She also brought back a deepened resilience and a livened passion for others. Later that summer she traveled to Beijing bound and determined to learn Mandarin. She returned once again with incredible photos and colorful stories of cultural experiences, adventures, adversity, independence and friendship. She has since gone on two more missions with OpSmile, each changing her life in the most profound ways. The earlier setback was a beautiful setup for what was already written in God's plan for her.

In August 2017 we drove the 500 miles to bring Austin to college. I looked at the young lady in the driver's seat and I saw courage. I nestled into my thoughts and willingly let her go. Before leaving her dorm room, I placed this poem that I had written for her underneath her pillow.

The heavens opened gently and delivered a gift
One like no other
She was peaceful
Curious eyes
so blue, so deep
drawing you in
landing inside your own mind
wondering what this child will bring

She brings love, kisses, hugs and love guarded
She brings playfulness, imagination, quiet contemplation,
So much laughter
imaginary friends, fun friends, mean friends
forever friends

She brings determination, self-motivation,
dedication to so many others, dedication to conquer any challenge
Who knew—I knew
What I didn't know is that I would be so grateful that I saved her
handmade
"LOVE IN A BAG!"
and in my heart I stockpiled all of the kisses and hugs
she methodically placed on my cheeks, forehead, lips and palms
each and every morning before elementary school
What I didn't know is
how the love would change
The little-girl love on display would, without notice,
become something that I would have to feel floating around the periphery
of our presence
I knew to respect and appreciate it all the same
she unknowingly asked for space
she earned it
and I knew that in that space, she would bloom
She needed me—unknowingly? Not sure, it didn't matter
I was her tried and true
She wanted to go to the people that needed her help
She wanted to befriend amazing people from the far corners of the world
She wanted to put her eyes on and take away in her own thoughts and beliefs
the experiences that she needed to have
She came home
She needed to
She makes me better
She makes me proud
Today, I make her bed, though not at home
I know that this place, this time in her life, is hers
And as she rests her sweet head on her pillow
after a long day of studies
a fun night with friends

a Sunday of tailgating
or a day that challenges her very being
I will be with her
I will be in her heart
She will be in mine
I will be a better person for this gift sent down
on a day that I will never forget
She will be a better person because
she is loved.

CHAPTER 4

Crossing Over

TIME MOVES CONTINUOUSLY FORWARD, at times moving so fast that I wish it would slow down, and then there are times it suddenly veers and stops dead in its tracks. In 2014, my life was stopped in its tracks. I was fifty-two years old, and I had already spanned two years of unexpected transformation in my life because of waning friendships. I had been in a holding pattern of confusion for two years, but on this day, I was knocked out of my holding pattern and into certain closure.

It was early Sunday morning, a time when I loved to sit with the peace of the sunrise and the musical grace of the birds greeting the new day. But on that morning, just as I had for the past two weeks, I left behind life's beauty to help ease the pain of impending death.

I quietly closed the front door as I left so I wouldn't awaken my husband and daughter from their peaceful slumbers. There was no sense in circulating the pensive sadness of mine. The grief would spread soon enough.

Inside my car the air was thick. It clogged my breath and encapsulated me from the simplicities of the world passing by. The silence was deafening. It was time to go, time to be brave, time to palliate the trepidation that would surely arise in my mom's frail body once she saw the hospital bed and hospice nurses arrive at her home. Leaning my head back on the headrest, I asked God not only for strength but also for grace and assurance in my words and my actions. As I drove halfway along the causeway extending across the glistening bay, I looked up to find an old friend. *How is it that this skeleton of a pine tree that all but touches the sky like a needle has become a gauge of what is imminent in my life?* I wondered. The perch served on special occasions as a throne to the almighty and elusive bald eagle.

That day was a special occasion. There he was, up on his piney throne, delivering to me an invaluable message. I stopped the car. The air around me was much thicker than before. My throat was tight. Heat swelled through my body, pushing tears from my eyes. I was sure of the sign.

His yellow talons and beak were symbols for the strength that I would soon need to summon. His majestic white head and tail served as ardent reminders of the presence of the Almighty. His sculpted brown wings were an admonition to rise above myself and navigate the uncertain wind beneath me. His keen watchful eyes became a sign of perception. This was a call to arouse and gather my intuition and discernment as we converged upon this death, a fate seen and felt so differently by everyone. All of these virtues would be invoked and tested in me in the days to come and would see us through the final precious hours of a woman who lay helpless—a woman who gave me life.

With my beating heart, my story began in August 1962. My family was big and busy, everyone in motion, constantly moving. I was the baby of the family—the youngest of seven children. I watched them all.

I was the observer of the bustling stream flowing throughout our home.

Our cedar closet upstairs was my refuge. I still love the soothing smell of cedar to this day. The smell is as comforting to me as the smell of freshly bloomed lilacs that I devotedly cut from our bushes every spring to bring into my Catholic school to adorn the venerated shrine of our Lady of Loreto. I would drop my fragrant cuttings into the gazing pool that graced the blessed ground at the feet of the Virgin Mary. The sublime water was a mirror into the soul. I held such conflicting emotions about this place that was my school and my church. I spent a lot of my time there. In so many ways it was sacred and safe. A delicate spirituality was established in me there, an introduction to what I believed I should nurture and protect throughout my life.

The stone there resonated more in me than the flesh. The stone figures held a sanctity in my mind, and for them and what they represented I was grateful since some of the humans in this house of God turned out to be less than saintly. I remember standing before various statues of Jesus, the Virgin Mary and other saints, and they somehow spoke to me. I could feel the light radiating from them, inspiriting my body and soul like I was sinking into warm, powdery, sun-drenched sand. The surrounding air diffused a peace that ran through my veins, restoring any hope that was breached by the sanctimonious behavior of certain priests and nuns at our parish.

I made a decision early on that I would believe in what felt right to me. And when I watched the parish priest smack a fidgeting boy with the same hand that held the burning candle meant for the blessing of our young throats, I was not only frightened, but I also knew this was far from virtuous. And after seeing my brother John abruptly leaving our Catholic school after being hit by a nun, I wiped the tears from my eyes and my faith in these people from my heart. I began to wonder: *Does the book that they read from hold disparate words from the book that I read? Do the daily prayers that we recite and unending Bible readings not apply to members of this clergy?* The purity of all I believed was good about that place collided with the reality that existed there.

Once again, I was being shaped by reality. I was being sculpted by the cold, sharpened modeling knife of death. I've endured the end of life of those I love and adore and one that I never touched but have undoubtedly felt.

The death of a parent is different from any other death.

Dad passed away on November 10, 2014, in a hospital just a mile from my parents' home in Florida. The entire time he was in the hospital, Mom sat at his bedside, witness to the ventilator that gave him breath and his still body and shuttered eyes, yet she still believed that he was coming home. The doctors spoke the inevitable truth over the phone and in person, but she wouldn't hear it. He was coming home with her. The obvious truth was more than she could bear. Reality finally knocked so loud that she had no choice but to answer to the heartbreak. The love of her life was not coming home with her. My sisters and I took her home. I handled the arrangements Mom asked me to handle, sensing her need to process what had just happened alone. I sensed her need for quiet and privacy to lie in their bed or sit in her chair right next to his and will him back.

Granting her the solitude she deserved to process her grief, I made my way to the Orlando airport. Once I returned my rental car and passed through security, reality took over. I suddenly lost all control of my emotions. I sat on a bench most likely meant for employees in the back of a Starbucks stall. I sobbed uncontrollably for an indeterminate amount of time. I remember looking up through my swollen eyes at two young baristas that had sheer panic on their faces. It was time to move on.

When I got on the plane I was relieved to be in my seat knowing that the hum of the engines and the pressurized air in the cabin would soon drown out my thoughts and compress my flash of sudden grief. I had just gotten settled when I felt a tap on my arm. A man from across the aisle was asking me to switch seats with him. I had an aisle seat and he wanted it. *My dad just died; take my seat.* I didn't care where I sat. I just wanted the plane to get in the air and take me home to my husband and daughter. I got settled into my new seat and couldn't help but look at the man sitting next to me smiling gently as if to say, "It's ok." The stewardess brought me a glass of wine and nodded towards the man that I had just switched seats with. I looked back and thanked him.

Suddenly I remembered that just minutes before boarding the plane, I had been crying my eyes out. I'm sure they were red and swollen. No wonder the man seated next to me was so amiable. After I drank a few sips of my wine, as if that were an indication that I was now safe to approach, the man quietly asked if I was okay. I simply said, "My dad just died." My tears held. He kindly asked my dad's name.

"Thomas" I said. The gap between two strangers was closing. His kindness was just the support that I needed. We shared polite conversation about my dad and then our children and the schools they attended. He and his family lived in Norfolk—small world. There was a warmth and authentic compassion in that man. He reminded me of my dad. As the plane landed, he formally introduced himself and handed me his business card. I introduced myself and looked down at his card. My heart flushed with comfort; his name was Joe, and he was a State Farm insurance agent, just as my dad had been for forty years! The intended connection was made, and I felt the syncronicity and peace from the support of the Divine. Joe was a lovely, kindhearted and caring man, just like my dad.

The imminence of death could be seen in Mom's tired brown eyes and felt in the thick gray air that we shared. But right then it was not death that we would contemplate. We didn't have time. At that moment, life was the intended focus.

Mom turned eighty-seven just days after moving to Virginia from her home in Florida. We had to finish catching up on life. She didn't like to talk on the phone, and our family visits with her in Florida didn't grant us freedom from disturbance amidst the unabated motion of our large family flock. Any lone visits with Mom were typically spent grocery shopping, cooking, cleaning, and occasionally riding in the car for a lunch out. A simple outing demanded most of our energy, hers and mine, to get Mom in and out of the car. She didn't move well at the onset of the end, but getting her out was important, and she loved to ride through the small neighborhoods that sat on the lake.

During these visits she remained fairly shuttered. There was a boundary around her. I lived in the confines of it all of my life, but now it was stronger than ever. Mom was always the captain of our ship, and unless it was taking on water, we knew not to bother her, and small talk was certainly a bother.

My mom's life was coming to an end. At seventeen years old, my daughter, Austin, stood closer to death than she ever had. She was just seven years old when my husband's mother died—her nana. Sure, she felt the sadness and the emptiness of missing her nana, but the experience was colored with the lighthearted crayon of youth. Now, we felt death in the wind, and my teenage daughter was old enough to recognize the ominous signs. Death was definitely undeniable.

During the days leading up to my mom's death, my daughter visited after school and snuggled with her "Meme" as Mom lay in her bed waiting for God to take her. We all waited with her—the few children and grandchildren living near her in Virginia. Each of us had our own time with her. It wasn't an established schedule hanging on the refrigerator door; we simply and comfortably respected one another's time. She was our mother, our center. We stayed close by, orbiting around our center, coming around again and again with a memory or a story that we wanted to share with her.

While my daughter and mom exchanged stories, I made a pot of chicken soup. I knew that Mom wouldn't actually eat any of the soup, but I hoped that the simmering, soothing aroma would blanket her room and bring with it a fond memory and a bit of comfort—the same comfort that she ladled into our bowls over the years, subliminally bestowing the recipe upon us not only for the soup but more importantly for compassion. Stories floated out of the bedroom as the savory scent floated in, warming our souls with the consolations of life.

My sweet daughter and mother had shared many talks in the previous two months, seemingly without urgency. Now there was a race against time. My daughter spoke of her summer in China, painting a vivid picture of her lone exploration of a buzzing Beijing, its inner *hutongs*, the 798 Art District, the noodle shops, the Great Wall and her proficiency in bartering at the markets. Meme shared a weak smile, and her eyes glossed over with pride for her adventurous granddaughter. She said that Austin's courage to go alone to a foreign country at such a young age reminded her of her own mother, who was sixteen years old when she emigrated from Czechoslovakia to the United States.

When my mother's mother, Christine, got on the huge ship that would carry her across the sea to a new land, she was dressed in a traditional Czech folk dress. It was the finest outfit she owned, and she was determined to begin her new life with pride and grace. She carried a modest bag with a few belongings, and in her heart she held a loving vision of the family that she left behind. Unable to speak the language of the faraway land that would be her home once the ship set anchor at Ellis Island, she feared nothing and believed that she could do anything.

Hearing my mother recount this story for my daughter made me recall sitting on the sofa as a little girl asking my grandmother if she was scared making that long, lonely journey. In her thick Czech accent and broken but beautiful English she simply said that she didn't have a choice. She wanted a better life for herself, and she knew she had to come to America to fulfill her dreams. Her blue eyes held so much resolve, so much strength as she remembered acquiescing to the unknown. She said that she was certain that the benefits of this new life would dissolve any fear or loneliness.

I heard my mom remind her granddaughter that the two intrepid souls share the same birthday. The warmth I felt on the special day that Austin was born dropped right back into my heart as if it were that very day seventeen years ago. I felt such pride and comfort that they share the same beautiful, clear and courageous blue eyes.

As my mom ran an inventory of her life, my daughter listened intently. The stories she told are precious and would not be spoken from her lips again. We are left with our memories, as well as the hope that we will never forget the sound of her voice.

Mom wanted to hear more stories from her granddaughter. Maybe she sought solace in a story that could transport her to a colorful land humming with life and away from her aching body and impending silence. Eager to dull her pain, my daughter told her grandmother about the train that she took from Beijing to the outer provinces, and how the noisy, sweaty, bumpy chicken truck of a train brought them to the beauty, peace and fresh air of the rolling green hills of Xiahe. She told my mother how she discovered a graceful land filled with wandering yaks, beautifully painted prayer wheels, and native people with a measure of spirituality, compassion and peacefulness that the stunning land provided them. This land dropped something into my daughter. The change was palpable. She took it all in and filled her heart with this gift. When she returned home it was as if she glowed with the spirit and soul of that sacred place.

The omen so eloquently delivered to me by the bald eagle that morning spoke to the ultimate sacred place. *I am ready*, I thought. *I*

will take this journey with my dying mother as far as I can take her. We will go together until I must let go her hand so she can pass into her final and divine repose.

The hospice bed arrived soon after I did. The bed spoke the truth. I softened the obvious statement it made as it engulfed the room and certainly all hopes of turning back; as we gently carried her pallid body, I tried to point out the favorable aspects of the bed. I had to dig deep and rise above the obvious. I mentioned how nice it would be to raise the head of bed so she could look out the window at the pond and the gardens. I covered her with warm blankets and a beloved quilt made by her brave Czechoslovakian mother. The quilt carried the essence of love, exactly what we needed to comfort Mom and cover the austerity of the bed. I felt my grandmother's presence as I tucked the quilt snugly over my mom's shoulders.

She looked so tired. She told me that she wanted to sleep. I respected her wishes and used the time to go home and take care of everyday life. I looked at her before I left. Her eyes were closed. She seemed comfortable in that mooring place anchored between life and death.

The next morning brought my sweet dad's birthday. In my gut I knew that would be the day. They were married for sixty-two years before my dad passed, and she had been without him long enough. My daughter and I brought a chocolate cupcake and a candle to celebrate the love of her life. I'll never forget her weak but tender voice as she sang "Happy Birthday" to him. The love in her song showed me a vulnerability that I had never seen in her, and blowing out the candle with the little breath she had left showed her determination to connect to him.

As the morning stretched on she became tired again. We left knowing she needed to regain her strength for visits from her other children and grandchildren sprinkled throughout the day.

In the early evening my heart suddenly started to race. I felt very unsettled. Something was wrong. I called my mom's nurse and was relieved when she said that my mom was resting just fine. I hung up and took a deep breath. A few minutes later, the phone rang; it was like a fire alarm had sounded off, shaking my entire home. My heart sank when the nurse said that my mom's breathing had suddenly changed and had become very labored and thick. My daughter and I ran out the door. On the way, I called the rest of the family; I was grateful to God that we were all only five minutes away.

When I arrived, the nurse was holding my mom's hand, and she had already called for the hospice charge nurse to come with medication. Mom's breathing was so strained and heavy it forced her abdomen up and out into a large mound as if her thick breath were angry at being stuck.

I kneeled beside her bed and looked directly into her eyes. The fear in her eyes was chilling. She whispered to me, "I can't breathe." I did the only thing that I knew to do. I kept our eyes connected, gently rubbed her forehead and assured her that she was breathing.

"You are breathing, Mom; just slow it down."

"I am?" she asked, and then she whispered to herself, "I'm breathing, I'm breathing."

She had such resolve. She always did.

"It's ok, Mom, just close your eyes and try to feel calm. We're all right here with you." Beautifully, at that moment the rest of the family arrived. A sense of calm came over her. She was not alone.

Her eyes closed for a few minutes. I stayed kneeling and connected to her and her breath, watching her eyes, wiping her mouth and feeling the surrender. I was sure she felt some comfort hearing the quiet conversations of her children and grandchildren who surrounded her bed. A few moments later she opened her eyes. They had somehow changed. I could see forever in them. Her breathing became terribly heavy. The room became silent amidst the amiable chatter of family.

Our connection became consuming. I felt her breath inside of me. It happened so fast—this spiritual alignment. I held her hand tighter and kept my eyes immersed in hers. Her eyes pleaded with mine. I reassured her with the calm conveyed to me that I would stay with her to the end. I felt the gradual shedding of her physical body. I felt God's presence on my shoulders. I could see a white light. It didn't simply surround my mother. It seemed to envelope both of us. We were inside of it. My voice was clear and uplifting. I smiled with love and assurance as I spoke to her.

"It's ok, Mom, you can go. Go to the light, Mom. Go, go to it. Can you see the light, Mom? Follow it. Mom, there's Dad; he's waiting for you! He has three red balloons! Can you see the balloons? Oh, Mom, there's Paul! He's standing! He's reaching his hands out for you, Mom!" I wanted so badly to reach my hands to his, I missed him so much, but this embrace wasn't for me. "He's here! He's wiggling his fingers; he's ready for you! Dad is smiling! He's so happy to see you! Follow the light, Mom."

"She's gone," I whispered, breaking the conversation that I could once again hear.

"What?" my sister said in shock.

Tears flowed from the faces across the bed from me. I looked back at the hospice nurse and smiled. She smiled back. She knew. There was never time to administer medication. Mom's passing was pure and free.

I had just experienced one of the most beautiful moments of my life. I felt incredibly warm and calm, filled with the tender guidance of my brother, the impassioned devotion of my dad, the restful soul of my departed mother and the loving presence and finishing grace of God.

CHAPTER 5

We Are the Steps We Take

MY MOTHER'S DEATH BROUGHT me to life—my life. I did not see this transformation coming. I didn't expect it and I didn't ask for it. But a strong spiritual influence swept in and set the change in motion at a distinct turning point in my life. I felt a guiding presence within and around me, but I had no idea how it would gracefully bring me to settle into myself once again. When I experienced spiritual guidance and support in the past, the focus was limited. This time I was being influenced to index my entire life—past, present and future—and discern what would stay, what must go and where I would ultimately settle. One day I felt it take over my body and soul like a team arriving to clean up after a natural disaster. My life had certainly not been a disaster, but a cleanup was needed. My thoughts cracked wide open, and I couldn't resist strolling through them.

I will never forget the vision that I saw before me while walking through my home one morning not long after my mom passed away. Any and all thoughts from my "to-do" list and the discord of settling my mom's estate vacated my mind, allowing space for the wisdom about to drop in. The vision was so metaphorically pure—of a taupe-colored, satin ribbon cinched with tucks along the circle it formed, and fastened together by a soft bow. Gently, and in slow motion, the tucks released and the bow untied. The ribbon delicately floated to the ground like a feather. I felt the clarity, the urge to move forward and let go of the past. I felt such gratitude for this delicate yet profound message. It was as if I was being given permission to release all that was fastened so tightly to me, buttoning up the soul deep inside that was patiently waiting to be set free. I no longer had to hold the family circle together, keeping it neatly tucked and afloat. My work was done, after all. My commitment was to my mom and dad, and now they were both gone.

A peace diffused throughout my body. I welcomed the calm with shuttered eyes and a deep, cleansing breath. Little did I know this would be the calm before the storm.

Choosing to release the past and let go of anything that prevents growth is not easy. While growth is important, it's not always our first choice. And sometimes we choose to grow out of order. It was time for me to change my direction, and this was now obvious to me. It was time for me to be completely present in my own life. I could finally plot the path to my future knowing full well that I would not be the sole navigator of my journey. I was being guided by something bigger than me. I trusted this guidance and I trusted my decision to let go. We are the steps we take. I felt relief in knowing that a change was coming. I was ready to walk forward.

It wasn't until I acknowledged my discomfort with my present self that I realized that my walk to and with myself had begun. I would not turn back despite the discomfort. This inventory inside of me has filled the shelves of my life, but not all of it makes up who I am.

In fact, so much of it was preventing me from being me. I soon became comfortable feeling uncomfortable. I knew that until I swept through my entire life and pulled out the stagnation from the hidden corners, I would never become clear. I wanted to be clear. In storing negative thoughts about myself and others, I was creating separation from the truth. I wanted to live in the clarity of truth rather than the obscurity of assumption.

When these shifts were set into motion, I really didn't know my place. I didn't know exactly what I was supposed to be doing right away. But I did know that I didn't like how I felt, and I knew I wanted the change. I knew that my heart hurt and I was the moving force to restore my life. The more I uncovered and the more that floated to the surface of my mind, the clearer it became that the hurt I was holding was self-inflicted. I was hanging on to all that wasn't working any longer instead of letting go of my expectations of others. It was time to let go of fears, judgement, and stories that I was telling myself. It was time to let go of relationships that had run their course. These emotions were mine, and they had taken over my life and my peace. The emotions that made me uncomfortable were buried treasures full of healing energy, truth and unseen potential. Inquiring into and finally releasing my limiting beliefs allowed the life that was waiting for me to appear.

It's so compelling to me how challenges continue to show up in our lives, stoking our awareness of the work that we have left to do. Without doing the work, nothing goes away. "Stuck" energy is powerful and unrelenting. I came to see that the shortcomings in others that made me uncomfortable were actually shortcomings in myself. The truth can be discomforting. I was determined to release the ghost of illusion and walk into the freedom of reality.

As I settled into contemplation of the hearts and images of those I felt had hurt me, I dispelled my assumptions and reversed the responsibility. I let go of the fear and pain, and I felt pure gratitude for the lessons that surfaced in my own life from those relationships. I came to understand that each one of us did the best that we could do with what we knew at the time. Now, I see that within *me* is the answer. I know that I am forever by my side and that *I* am my only solution.

To honestly feel and inquire into the void left in my life from my mom's death and friendships that unraveled was a conscious choice. I spent my days alone in the unconditionally loving company of my three dogs and the solitude of nature. It was in the stillness that the thoughts would come one by one and sometimes over and over, just in case I didn't fully grasp the teachings the first few times. Each thought exposed the pieces of my life that needed to be revealed in their true form.

I was taking an early morning walk on my fifty-third birthday, dogs in tow. It was mid-August. The air was sticky with summer's thick heat. When I turned the corner, seemingly on cue and waiting for my arrival and attention, a huge cluster of leaves fell across my path in slow motion. It was as if they had decided to freely let go of summer before the cool air and angry winds of fall and winter's pending storms forced them down. Being naturally guided, I too made this choice. I chose to let go.

This wasn't the only time I watched the leaves let go. Nature continued to guide, remind and support me over the following weeks with one deliberate landing after another, leaves strategically dropping into my path. What I no longer needed fell away from me, allowing new growth and, most importantly, allowing the light in. As Winston Churchill once said, "Solitary trees, if they grow at all, grow strong."

I had a choice. I knew what I needed to do, but I was still holding on tight while simultaneously trying to let go. Holding on can be so much easier than letting go. It doesn't require any delving into one's soul. But what we may not realize is that holding on means a constant recovery of old habits. A recycling of the stagnant over and over into every cell, every relationship and every spoken word, presenting unhealthy relationships, unhealthy views of ourselves and often physical illness. "Inner freedom doesn't come from control, it comes from having the courage to let go of what isn't working in your life" were the words pushing me forward and repeatedly visiting my thoughts. But before untangling completely, a recall was in order.

There were things that I couldn't walk away from. I made a commitment to myself, and in order for this renovation of my soul to be pure I had to own my previous behavior. I needed to own what made me uncomfortable.

Each of us plays a part in everything that happens in our lives. To realize and nurture this facilitates growth, forgiveness and freedom. I needed to call to mind my part in all of my relationships. The lull in my life from my mother's death and an overall transformation of friendships created a place for what was broken to show clear. I wasn't proud of my past random and reckless words that I sorely mistook as playful or honest. I needed to reflect on how I had left other people's hearts. I felt the call to not only confess my behavior but also to apologize to the friends that I had hurt. From regret comes apology. From apology, forgiveness, and from forgiveness comes peace. The vulnerability I honored while apologizing was cleansing, and I felt it in the pit of my stomach. My regret was authentic and it was mine. Whether or not my apology was accepted, I felt a release and the permission to forgive myself. My heart was healing. I realized that I was not trapped in my current life. I was free to change.

I was breaking free and coming back to the self I had moved so far away from. My wandering was over.

Kinetically freewheeling through life was no longer an option. I needed to become fully conscious and aware of where I was spending my days and who I was spending them with. I returned to my heart center and felt a longing to spend time there, alone, and do the work.

"If we do now make our atonement well,
our peace will, like a broken limb united,
grow stronger for the breaking."

—William Shakespeare, *Henry IV*

Around this time is when I realized I had given so much of myself away in friendships and family relationships. I also realized just how much of me was gone. When the unraveling of friendships and some family relationships began, I felt a burning pain in the pit of my stomach. My heart was severed. I was forced to look down the barrel of my loaded past and pull the trigger to release the smoke and fire. And this release would not come without distress. Changing myself, not the world, was my work at hand. My role was the only one that I could define, critique and learn from.

At night, I lay in bed silenced by the darkness. My insides ached with emptiness. The pain filled the hollows of my stomach and echoed in the anxious quiet of my mind. I learned a lot during those sleepless nights. I don't want to go back there. And not going back there meant turning toward what I disliked in myself and in my life. This was an uncompromising and difficult examination, but nothing worth having is ever easy.

What I discovered pushed me forward. I realized what I am made of and who I am. I found myself and I found my grace, pulling me toward my future. My strength showed up to carry me forward. After several months of feeling forsaken and dazed, I saw the gift in what I had earlier perceived as desertion of friends, and I found an awakening in what I labeled as disloyalty of some family members.

Versifying the disintegration of the friendships in a dark recounting would be forfeiting the grace that I have come into. My friendships' endings might sound very similar to anyone that has experienced the fall of a friendship, and since the blanks can be filled in with personal experiences by you, the reader, I am honoring what was good in each past relationship and choosing not to let condemnation in. As they say, the devil is in the details. Everything certainly happens for a reason, and I began to see this as a remarkable understatement. I became grateful to those very people for the resulting reward of turning to myself for the first time in a very long time. I needed a holistic biopsy and I was undergoing just that.

I realized that the hurt needed to be fierce to garner my attention. God wanted my sustained concentration. My life was exploding to meet itself. It was the unrelenting shrapnel of the death of my mom, the dissolve of family dynamics, friendships that were hanging by a string and the invites that never came. Everything happened at once. The bullets kept coming at me at full speed, pulverizing the person that I had become and exposing a raw platform for me to examine and inquire into all that was holding me back and obscuring my vision. I couldn't ignore or go around this force. I had to go straight through the fire to get to my soul.

I was ready to remove what had corroded in me and restore my life with the peace and love that I deserved. I grounded myself in the bubble of stillness. I stood in the forgiveness and warmth of the morning sun, in the graceful afternoon breeze and before a luminous moon, talking to myself and to God. I was grateful for this magnificent peace. This simple path became my saving grace, my renewed state of mind, my Kingdom Come! Only I had the power to unlock the healing process. There was something worth having beyond this pain. I could almost touch it.

∞

I soon discovered that in serenity, gifts abound. On a quiet day while gardening, a question dropped into my placid mind like a drop of water on a still lake: "What would your angel whisper in your ear?" I quickly went indoors, found a pen and paper, and wrote down these words in a matter of moments.

You are good enough.
Look for the light in the corners.
I wish you peace.
Believe that you deserve it.
Come with love and harmony and ask the same of others.
Reach deep inside and listen.
Cultivate and nurture your ability to listen,
Share a glance, add a smile.
Walk with an open heart full of light and love.
Reach deep inside yourself.
Welcome the past—understand it—let it go.
Get it out of your way.
Don't look back.
Pray.
Be a lovely friend.
Imagine the most amazing vision of yourself.
Bring your vision to life.
Love who you are.
I will be here every step of the way.

When I finished writing these ethereally delivered words, I read them over and over again. Every word and every meaning found a safe place in my soul. This angel of mine was truly with me, within me and around me. My heart felt full with light and love. I felt supported and guided.

Because of this experience, my awareness was roused. The door to my consciousness cracked open even further—its flame burned steady in my mind. I was just thoughts away from changing my life. My path was clear, and I stood still upon it, poised and ready for the gentle wisdom to find its way to me. I moved forward manifesting and emanating the love and grace that was bestowed upon me. In my awareness, I came back to my true self. I saw the heartache for what it honestly was and I embraced the lessons.

There are surface reasons that caused this friendship to end, but I choose to focus on the deeper wisdom. From each season of our lives comes growth, just as in the natural world. Friendships and other relationships sometimes shift. In the realignment, these relationships looked and felt very different. I began to love these friends from a distance. I wanted to start the purification process and give these relationships the dignity they deserved. After all, they were a huge part of my life for more than twenty of my (then) fifty-six years. I set the bad memories free.

Moving forward with my family, I decided to occupy a different space, other than the one I had unconsciously settled into for so many years. The space had to be sacred; I had to be stronger than I was. And in this strength and peace, I knew I would emerge more composed and resolute.

I would respect the differences in our journeys. I would respect the difference of our places in time. I felt a welcoming space for new friends. I felt love for the friends that I moved on from, and was able to love them for everything that they taught me. I saw that there were so many redeeming qualities in each of these friends, and we had made so many joyous memories. I felt the beginning of my life. I felt love all around me, although not in all of the usual places. My heart was now clear and open and filled with the beautiful love that had held me through the storm, and it was time for me to reciprocate by sending the love out into the world.

It is with our hearts that we give and receive love. The heart is the center of our emotions. I have felt sorrow in my heart from loss. I have felt pain in my heart from malevolence. I have felt fear in my heart from isolation.

My heart had a literal hole in it. I was born just like everyone else with an opening in my heart, but mine never closed. For years, I lived with a hole in my heart. What amazed me was how the hole began to cause me health problems for the first time just as the bottom fell out of friendships and family relationships and after my mother passed away.

The first sign of distress came during a workout class. I became very short of breath and blacked out for a few moments. I went directly to the hospital. The next step was a transesophageal echocardiogram, a test that produces pictures of the heart. I found a great cardiologist and was retested every six months to monitor the size of the hole. The weakness in my heart continued to show up with bouts of pneumonia and exhaustion. Looking back, it was no surprise: my mom had died, I missed my friends, and I was purging so many raw emotions. Just eighteen months after her death, my doctor informed me that it was time to close the hole—it had gotten dangerously larger.

This closure was purely symbolic to me. I didn't interpret the condition or the procedure as medical. I didn't alert family and friends, with the exception, of course, of my husband and daughter. Even to them, I downplayed the procedure. The closure was a gift delivered at the perfect time in my life, and this gift was mine to cherish. Just before and after the closure I found myself smiling with accomplishment. My heart was cleansed of the heartache and grief and now it would be whole. I didn't want to distort this renewal of my heart and surrender to the medical diagnosis. There was so much more here. I had worked honestly and assiduously for the past three years, and I saw this triumph for everything that it truly was: letting go and letting love in.

Learning to walk away with clarity and grace was an extraordinary evolution in my life. It didn't just happen with the snap of my fingers. I had to receive and discern all of the things that brought me to that place of dissolve. I had to admit to myself that the connections were waning. I had to recognize that the harmony that once fed and protected these relationships was fading and taking on a new form. As relationships changed and I made a commitment to release my past and accept my future, I consciously settled in the words of Rumi: "'You'll not have escaped from yourself until your light is a thousand times you.' I could not know what he meant before he exploded me."

As time passed, my heart healed and my awareness peaked. I began seeing myself in the undesirable habits of others. This realization brought relief. The struggle and the judgement were soon gone. Seeing the flaws as mine left me fully open to accept the other person with compassion, knowing that each of us walks our own paths in our own varied time. I now felt a distinct tenderness toward those I once felt uncomfortable around. We are all alike in so many ways; we're all learning, discovering and evolving.

My heart is open and it feels so much bigger than it was; it feels pure and unshakable. My love for past friends feels like just love, nothing else. Relationships that once bruised my heart have taught me to love bigger, listen harder and feel more—no conditions or expectations, no fine print, just love, lucent and real.

Despite the refitting of my life, I chose to keep my heart open and nourish the peace that came with the deep acceptance. By respecting that our progress and our journeys differ, we become free from forming opinions of others. And in this space of respect and understanding we make room for love. Have faith in what will soon be. Be patient for the life that is on its way to you. Walk toward the arms that celebrate you and value you. They're out there and they're wide open. My load is lighter now. It is worth carrying—it's full of courage, love and wonder.

CHAPTER 6

Animal Medicine

NATURE, IN ALL ITS parables, beautifully illustrates and heightens life's truths and wisdom while graciously teaching valuable lessons and bringing the gift of inspiration to those that stand open in its illumination. To be grounded to the earth, witnessing the magical cycles of creation in nature, is to intimately encounter the discernible embodiment of the Divine. As an adult, when I found myself secluded in nature as I had when I was a young girl, the quiet felt oddly familiar. I had to welcome it back into my life and remember it in my soul. I had strayed so far from its expansive harmony that I stood in the eye of my own storm. I realized that I had been living as a character in everyone else's lives, and it was then that the winds whipped in to garner my attention and will me back. The slow and patient rhythm of nature became my healing field—a renewing space where I went in search of myself.

When there is loss, whether it's a friendship or the life of a loved one, first we see grief and only grief. Nature presents loss in a very different way. During the storm, trees bend and sway in the screaming, testing winds. Leaves are stripped from the limbs. When the air becomes still, the tree stands strong and tall, reaching for the light. Nature imparts upon all of us an understanding of life, but you must listen and follow its lead. It can teach us to reconcile with our own challenges by becoming more tuned-in and perceptive of what is truly at hand. There is an innate wisdom in the natural world, a sense of groundedness and attention to what is significant in life.

In coming back to myself, my first encounter with an obvious assigned lesson involved a huge snapping turtle. It was late June and I was driving home midmorning and had just turned onto my quiet, one-lane street. Clawing slowly across my path was a curiously large reptile. I stopped and got out of the car to realize that this wasn't the usual box turtle that I occasionally encountered. This snapper had a sharp pointed nose and folded, thick, brownish gray skin that resembled tumbled stone. His shell was gray and gritty with baked-on mud, looking like a steel helmet in need of a good shine. His leathery prehistoric legs and knife-like claws clenched the asphalt with no obvious intention to retract. His powerful jaw opened fiercely to let me know that he wasn't messing around. Typically nocturnal and rarely seen out of their aquatic habitat traveling across the land, he was my first and most explicit clue to begin the examination of my life. I patiently waited for him to cross the road and clear my path.

As much as I knew that this was indeed a sign, I didn't know what it meant. This unknown was an opening, an opportunity to curate. I reached out to my yoga teacher and dear friend, Angela. She and I have shared a comfortable and familiar connection from the first day that I visited her yoga studio. Her philosophy is reflective of her own studies and belief that yoga is a living tradition and a spiritual science that unites the body, mind and spirit. For over four decades, she has nourished herself and the students of her studio by her exemplary conscious lifestyle and expanding knowledge in spiritual development, breathwork and animal spirits, just to name a few. I was compelled to decipher the meaning of this message—Angela was the answer. She returned my email with an excerpt from the *Medicine Cards* book. I read how the turtle is the oldest symbol for planet Earth in Native American teachings, along with other engaging and very significant meanings. The meanings all correlated with my life, and as time passed, the metaphors were as clear as crystal.

The most poignant meaning to me was the understanding of protection. The earth's protection comes in the form of change, new growth and necessary alterations. There I was, with the edifying hands of the Universe placed upon my shoulders, pointing me in the direction of my learned path and in the direction of change and necessary alterations.

The next morning brought a reiteration of the previous day's lesson in case I didn't grasp the loaded meaning the first time around. I raised the shade on my front window, letting the morning light into the room and granting me my first glance of the world outside. I stopped in my tracks. There he was, the snapping turtle, in my driveway, which was a good 500 to 600 yards away from where we first met yesterday. I couldn't help but stand and stare and feel the inaugural turn of the key unlocking my soul.

Nature has an innate and beautifully calming ability to listen to us and command our undivided attention. Nature is fluid and welcoming, and forever at the perfect and precise juncture where one is compelled to step into it. A relationship with the natural world is incredibly powerful, and once you commit yourself to it, you find its sincere essence mesmerizing. With a deep understanding and realization of our true connection to all things, we can become virtuous, completely present and at peace. What we become from this contemplative connection, we graciously bring forth into the world.

At that time in my life, I found myself dissolving into the natural world. It became my spiritual alchemy. I became its chosen, obedient disciple, embracing its power and standing open to receive. I was connected to the intense spirit and all-encompassing essence of this teaching ground.

Albert Einstein once said, "The most beautiful and most profound emotion we can experience is the sensation of the mystical." Nature is an intoxicating mystery. The most esoteric bequests from the natural world are those that are unusual and so out of form that you know to shine a light on them.

A few months after the significant visits from the snapping turtle, I experienced another extraordinary visit. I was sitting in my backyard on a Sunday afternoon. The fall air was crisp, so the warm sun felt like a light blanket. Out of nowhere came what sounded like a train off in the distance. What made this sound odd is that we don't live anywhere near train tracks.

The sound of rolling thunder soon changed into a colossal chorus of chirps suppressing any and all sound in the vicinity. I looked up to a billowing black carpet that swept down and covered the trees surrounding me. The green turned to black; hundreds and hundreds of grackles eclipsed the leaves. I couldn't help but become mesmerized by this dense, elaborate exhibit, and as quickly as the birds came, they ascended in unison in acoustic murmuration. Their rhythmic vibration oscillated through me as they departed with the healthy hum of a well-oiled machine. I watched in amazement as their combined force enveloped me and left me feeling as though the intensity could lift me into their swirling sphere. They ambled west, turning and maneuvering into graceful shapes reminiscent of drifting jellyfish.

I had to leave this marvel behind. Life was calling. It was time to drive my daughter to meet another parent driving the girls to lacrosse practice. The dad shuttling the girls to practice was thankfully awakened to life's curiosities. I was excited to share. He smiled and said, "I believe you just received a blessing!" I was filled with joy. Like manna from Heaven, I took in the spiritual feast for all that it was meant to be.

When I returned home I opened my *Medicine Cards* book to discover that the grackle teaches to transcend the congestion of old emotions. The message was undeniable and timed precisely with that particular juncture in my life. I went on to read how emotions that are not handled and cleared could cause congestion in the body and in turn cause physical illnesses. I knew this and I knew that an emotional clearing was overdue. I had started the untangling, but this process wouldn't happen overnight. The assemblage of grackles was like my support group; they were letting me know that I was on track. They were phenomena of nature confirming my work at hand.

Indigenous elders have been relating with Mother Earth and all God's creatures for centuries. Mastering the virtue and intelligence in the messages, these elders hand down the gift of communicating with all living things, showing us that acquiring wisdom nurtures respect. Getting to know all creatures that you come into contact with not only gives you an opportunity to learn something new, but it opens the door to understanding the being rather than fearing it. This opening raises our consciousness and carries us along on our purposeful path. Go, walk down the road that you have not discovered, and lean in, feel yourself in close harmony with the natural world, and behold the higher powers awakening within you.

A simple but mindful walk outdoors can be so rewarding and even induce meditation. Allowing ourselves to be quiet and settled in on a walk is incredibly renewing, nourishing and powerfully healing. The natural world and the Divine recognize our loneliness, our fear and our pain. Give the message a chance to come. Our reward waits in the heightened connection only experienced in the stillness. You will see and hear nature communicate its understanding and impart upon you the ability to tap into your answers.

The nourishment of my soul continued. I remained accepting and in awe of every anomalous visit from each creature whose lesson connected with the prevalent work happening within me. I pulled into my garage one afternoon and got out of my car to hear something rustling about behind a cooler. I moved the cooler and met eyes with a snake. I went inside and called my husband, who was at work. When he was a teenager in the '60s, he was fascinated with snakes and would go into the state park to catch them and sell them to the local serpentarium. He was happy to come home and decipher the species as a king snake. He skillfully picked up the snake, got back into his car and brought it down the road to a densely wooded area. I picked up my *Medicine Cards* book to decipher my message.

The next morning as I walked past my glass front doors I noticed something dark on the front porch nestled right up against the threshold of the door. I stared in amazement through the glass. It was another snake. I made another call, and in his analysis of that day's snake, my husband determined that it was a female king snake perhaps looking for her mate. After carrying her upstairs to show our daughter our serpent friend, he got back into his car and brought the female to the same wooded area. They were reunited, and I was, in turn, becoming reunited with myself.

To the Native Americans, a snake represents transformation and healing. Before shedding its skin, a snake's eyes cloud over and only become clear again after its old skin has been shed. I was eager to release the pallid aspects of my life and see the world anew. My eyes had been clouded over for long enough. I was grateful for the clarity returning to my life. I became absorbed in the thought of how competent our Universe is and how the very value of nature for all of us lies in finding the Divine and finding ourselves. I cannot imagine a more beautiful or noble place in which to search.

Nature's tutelage continued to propel my renewal. Gifts kept coming, each one bearing a distinct message. It was up to me to decide whether it was time to learn. I welcomed nature's unparalleled healing in which I had found a new companion and confidant.

On a beautiful blue-sky day, I was missing my severed friendship and feeling lonesome in a way that seemed to suck the life out of me. I had just returned from the gym, and as clear as the sky was just outside of my window, my thoughts were heavy with uncertainty and conflict. These wavering thoughts showed up in the beginning of my self-exploration, but each time, something extraordinary would happen to override my fruitless thinking. This day was one of those exceptional days.

My dogs began barking and ran to the door leading to the backyard. They barked so relentlessly that I knew something was out there for me to see. I walked out back alone, leaving the spritely chorus inside. I looked up to the tree that framed many of the directives presented to me. There were seven great blue herons statuesquely perched on the alpine limbs of our pine tree. This was something I had never seen. I had seen many lone blue herons on various occasions, but never had I seen seven flocked together in such a rare assembly.

Heron medicine speaks of self-discovery, acknowledging your weaknesses with truth, building inner strength and facing all thoughts and emotions. It also speaks of self-reliance and following one's own path without the need for a lot of people around—somewhat of a loner existence. I'm not sure the message could have been any clearer, more affirming or more reassuring of the need to have this time alone. I also referred to my *Numerology and The Divine Triangle* book by Faith Javane and Dusty Bunker.

> The number 7 Seeks Answers. It tries to establish a philosophy by which to live and attempts to penetrate the mystery behind its existence, which it has never questioned to this point. Because solitude is necessary for analysis, the 7 feels the need to spend time alone,

away from the crowds, in touch with nature. It looks for friendship with those of an elevated consciousness that can match its own. And on the seventh day God rested. All things rest under the 7 because time is needed in which to think. The ions under 7 feel poised and calm; they realize that they now need to be still and to know.

Once again, I felt truly supported. And just like that, my mind became as clear as the sky above.

In January 2017, during a huge snowstorm, which is not common for coastal southeastern Virginia, seventeen enormous white pelicans buoyantly floated into the small cove off of our backyard and took up residence for a week. They were absolutely fascinating to watch. The poise of these creatures in mid-air was beautiful, especially in the pink light of dawn. The pelicans that typically fly in and out of our area are grayish brown with a bill to match. The group of seventeen was as white as the snow falling around them. Their bills were a bright orange that turned the pink hue of a summer sunset when the flurry-filled sky cleared. I have never seen this type of pelican—the American white pelican—near our home.

It is one of the largest birds in North America with its nine-foot wingspan. Their feathers were so downy and white they reminded me of angel wings, especially when they were gracefully opened into their glorious spans. When the wind howled across the water, the flock tightly nestled together, burying their bills into each other's plumage. This sight was so beautiful and peaceful I felt it in my heart—another exquisite gift to awaken my senses. When the flurries gave way to warming sunshine, the velvety creatures emerged from their huddle and took to the sky. The pageantry of the soaring, diving and wheeling of this collection of majestic creatures was a sight to behold. They were dancing on air!

This was the most estimable entertainment possible. Seeing them thrust back their wings, point their huge bills like a laser toward the water and dive in after a fish was quite an engaging display as well. At rest, they formed a long, single line in the frigid water, staying afloat until effects of the winter storm passed. Sharing the frigid repose of their weeklong stay stirred another awakening to yet more symbolism in my life. Despite some solemn and uncomfortable emotions, I will stay afloat and with sharpened focus continue to delve into the depth of my feelings. The water is a symbol of emotions. The pelican reminds us to rise above our emotions through growth and stay buoyant despite the weight of life's challenges.

As time passed, four crows became my guardsmen. My three dogs were always on alert, as dogs are, but since they spent a lot of time inside the house, additional surveillance was apparently needed to keep me aware of visits from the wild things that I looked forward to. The black-winged foursome could cause quite a commotion, and once I discovered the riches in their clatter, I looked forward to it. Their territorial caws were my signal to grab my camera and admire the guests waiting outside my door.

The bald eagle impelled the crows' most raucous behavior. When I stepped outside onto their stage, the lustrous black foursome would show their stuff by taking turns taunting the eagle, zipping and cutting into its space. The others would perch on nearby limbs, strategically surrounding what they deemed an intruder while dipping and bobbing as if to music. This act only lasted a few moments, and the crows would fly off and leave me in peaceful admiration of the white-headed, powerful creature. I soon became accustomed to the eagle's high-pitched shrill, so if the crows were off on an escapade, I knew when the eagle was near and I would follow its call. The call would pull me to his chosen location, tugging at my thoughts to unravel the message. In animal medicine, the eagle represents the power of the Great Spirit, the sacred connection to the Divine. I felt the sacred power with every visit from this extraordinary creature and a shivering of my spine with every high-pitched call.

For months while my elderly neighbor fought to recover from a debilitating fall, two adult bald eagles would perch in the tree on their property. Whether I was driving home from errands or working in my garden, the two would do a flyover to let me know that they were taking their post. After my sweet neighbor succumbed to her injuries and unexpectedly passed away, the eagles kept watch. After a few months my neighbor's husband moved to Maine to be closer to his children. That was the last I saw of the eagles in their tree.

It was not, however, the last I would see of the bald eagle altogether. In fact, I documented twenty-one straight days of distinguished visits. Most encounters were at or near my home, but they showed up at unconventional locations too, like on the interstate. Some days, I was graced with two or three separate visits, and other days two or three would alight at the same time.

One of the most extraordinary and commanding communions with this magnificent creature was on a beautiful midwinter morning. A lone eagle settled in my tree in the backyard and charged the early morning hours. I grabbed my camera and shot a few frames of my friend enjoying the break of day. I continued out into the yard with my dogs, enjoying my morning tea, thankful my camera was slung over my shoulder. Without notice, four bald eagles circled the sky above me. I moved down into the grass; they followed and dropped in so close above my head I could feel the wind beneath their wings. The sight was so exquisite and profound; warmth melted over my body and almost brought me to my knees. A sudden breeze blew across my face. I was standing on the altar of nature's cathedral.

"Only by its roots does a tree stand tall, and only by its own light does the sun shine brightly and bring life to our world. So it is with you, only when you're trusting, loving and rooted in your true self, will the life that is your highest potential begin to manifest. Only when you are walking on the path of your highest potential will you ever be able to shine brightly and bring light to the darkness of others."—Anonymous

CHAPTER 7

An Angel Takes Flight

WHAT IS A GIFT? What feeling or imagery does this word bring forth in your mind when you give it thought? I'm guessing that your own life and you yourself may not come up. A gift isn't always wrapped in beautiful paper with a matching bow. And many of us don't realize the value of our own unique offerings. There is a source of abundance within each one of us, and we are meant to unwrap it and extend it to the world. Mother Teresa left the gift of these beautiful words as a reminder: "May you not forget the infinite possibilities that are born of faith in yourself and others. May you use the gifts that you have received, and pass on the love that has been given to you."

Every new day brings with it a fresh opportunity for each of us to renew, unfold and love who we are. Once we learn to love ourselves, extending that glorious love becomes second nature. Nurture the compassion that already exists within you. Draw it out. The finest endowment of all is the love that we have to give. We are here to give it and we are here to receive it. As we learn to cherish and cultivate a warm heart, our love permeates, and everyone in our world receives our loving essence. By simply recognizing, respecting and sharing what we have been blessed with, we manifest our gratitude before

God and Universe for our favor, and it is in this humble gratitude that our souls are reciprocally inspirited and our loving energy expands. As Amelia Barr once shared, "Let me tell thee, time is a very precious gift of God, so precious that he only gives it to us moment by moment."

Your talents and offerings to this world don't have to be extraordinary. The smallest gifts are often the most powerful. And the most profound and remarkable offerings are those that we don't often give ourselves credit for. Unearth your bounty; someone is waiting to feel your blessing. Realize your beautiful riches, and share them. Whether you realize it or not, you can affect someone's life. You are someone's miracle. Ultimately, you will experience fulfillment in yourself by helping those around you experience love. Your gift doesn't have to be grand, but please, don't let it be nothing. Someone out there needs what you have been blessed with.

The gifts in my life have been plentiful. Even when a circumstance did not appear to be positive, a heartfelt bequest later appeared. I see every adversity, challenge, loss and pain as a valuable gift. These lessons, although agonizing and intense, have sculpted who I am. I am finally comfortable in my bones and grateful for every lesson that has inspired growth.

I like to remember that everyone we come in contact with each day is fighting his or her own conflict—big or small. And rather than ignore the presence of another person, stranger or not, a kind smile is a simple offering that might open hearts. I have encountered people here and there—usually strangers, but at times a friend, family member or an acquaintance—and I see myself in their anger or their pain. The look on their face or the slip of their tongue takes me directly back to a time in my life when I looked or behaved that way. I recall and converge upon a quick case history of my own battle. The live journal plays back in my thoughts as I stand palpating every emotion that I felt at that time. I then come back to this person before me with an open heart with hopes to ease their pain even if all I can offer them is simply to understand.

Understanding is a gift that we extend in goodwill to those that need us—those that need to feel that they are not alone and not the one single person on this earth that has ever felt this anguish or reacted in a less than graceful manner. By becoming aware of each other's strengths and weaknesses, we move past being tolerant and we become accepting by seeing ourselves in the very human qualities that we are all trying to polish and improve. With understanding, awareness and acceptance, hearts open.

Listening is an act of love. It is a gift that is bestowed upon both parties—the speaker and the listener. We learn so much more from listening than we do from talking. Sitting back and truly listening is grounding and enlightening. Listening nourishes us. There is a lot to learn in the nuance. We give so much when we are patient and silent. This silence is love. When people come to us in confusion or discontent, the power in expressing their issues out loud is healing in and of itself. Not everyone is looking for us to solve his or her problems; simply listening might be all that they need.

Leave your thoughts. Be present with your heart. Becoming a good listener takes discipline and composure. It also takes practice. Not everyone wants to hear our story or have us compare our similar experience. They want us to hear *their* story. And as much as their problem may resemble ours, it isn't the same; their problem is theirs alone, right then and in that moment. Show love and respect for the person by listening intently and actually feeling their story. Resist the urge to rehash your similar narrative. You have most likely already told your story to a friend who kindly listened and allowed you the space to let it go.

Mastering the ability to listen with an open heart is one of the most beautiful gifts that you can give to yourself. You diffuse calm through your presence when you no longer sit ready to pounce on the end of the other person's sentence and when your thoughts are no longer meandering and foraging for your next comment. Sincerely receiving the words and emotions of others manifests true love and understanding. I can't think of a more radiant emotional endowment. There is no better gift than complete presence.

A handwritten soulful note is one of my favorite gifts to receive. I have been lucky enough to share inspiring correspondence with a few very special people who still practice the art of letter writing—using a pen and paper to speak from their hearts. The gift of reflective letter writing has taught me the joy in receiving such thoughtful exchanges and how much joy can be found in composing an intimate response.

I have saved many of the beautiful letters I have received over the years, and I'm grateful to have them. Some of my elderly friends are not able to write any longer or they have passed on. I miss their stories and hearing their voices as I read through their beautiful encounters in life. Rereading them now is a warm reminder of how special this correspondence is to me. In thoughtful writing a true character is revealed. Reading another's account is like listening to a melody inside the mind and soul of the writer. There is such beauty in collecting our thoughts and recreating our stories. This recollection gives us the space to appreciate and find honest gratitude in our lives, especially in its mundane simplicities. And with this gratitude, the words that you compose are delivered from your heart onto the paper, and they travel across the country or around the world to deliver inspiration, insight and love.

The angel I painted after my brother's death was a gift to me, directly from the angels above and around me. I accepted this gift with an open heart, and with that open heart, the light and information came to me. I knew that this painting was special, and I wanted to share its beautiful energy. I had copies made of the ethereal painting, knowing that one day I would share this spirit of peace with someone that needed it.

That very day came after reading a series of articles in my local newspaper, *The Virginian-Pilot*. "A Chance in Hell" was published in 2011 after reporter Corinne Reilly and photographer Ross Taylor devoted two weeks of their lives at the NATO hospital in southern Afghanistan. They brought home the reality of war to those of us that have no real concept—I felt the souls of the wounded and the souls of the healers within me.

A new article in the series came each morning over a period of five days. Each story left me sitting in my chair with tears rolling down my cheeks, sick with the horrifying and lonely reality of war. The following mornings brought a longing for the next story and the next photos to draw me in closer to a world that I now realized deserved my utmost respect and compassion. Every report left me feeling the need to reach out and offer a flicker of light into even the smallest corner of the war-torn life that I read about.

Everyone should read this series of articles, or at least one like it. This compilation of real-life stories brought me as close as I could come to slipping into the lives of those on the front line. I was transported to the Role 3 medical treatment facility at the Kandahar Airfield, envisioning the medics, doctors, nurses and soldiers as they stood on the altar hanging between life and death. Having a raw understanding of their reality and striving to see into their lives inspired me to love a little more and cast my net a little wider.

A few months after reading "A Chance in Hell," I carefully cut the canvas from the wooden frame and rolled my angel painting to fit into a long mailing tube that would make the journey to a world that I now had a heartbreaking glimpse of. It was the only way I could reach these people that I now felt a connection to. This was my way of casting a glimmer of hope and love, the same hope and love that my angel brought to me years ago. I wrote a short letter explaining the meaning and creation of my painting and how it brought me such peace and comfort after losing my brother Paul, and how I hoped that it would bring a bit of peace, comfort, love and strength to everyone there.

To my surprise, about two months after sending the painting on its way, I received an email. My angel had arrived in Afghanistan, and upon unrolling the canvas, the officers were struck by the angel's purple heart and knew immediately where she would stand guard. I was so moved when I learned that they had the painting framed. This was another example of my detachment from the reality there. I had no idea that such a frame could be found in Afghanistan.

The frame that they chose was inlaid with purpleheart wood, an exotic wood also known as peltogyne or amaranth. I'm guessing that they chose this wood for the frame not only because it complemented the purple color of my angel's heart but most importantly because of the significance of a Purple Heart in their military world. My heart stopped when I read this. The pure dedication and commitment to honor that ran through the veins of every man and woman serving there was so noble and so palpable. Above the painting rests a beautiful handmade wooden sign that reads *Fallen Angels*, and to its side hangs a poem for the fallen.

One of the soldiers later wrote to me saying that she likes to believe that the angel will be watching over the fallen soldiers on their way home. I believe this with all my heart.

There are currents in life that connect us. These currents are constant. We can join in at any time and at any crossing. Let yourself be carried to the heart of another. There is no such thing as distance if we simply close the gap. We are all closer to each other than we think. Reach out and take your magic and grace somewhere there isn't any. We must commit to care for one another and to help mend each other's hearts.

I am astounded by the miracles in my life. I don't regard them as coincidence or luck. Instead I see them for what they truly are: miracles. In every heartbreak shines a blessing. I wade through the challenges of life to discover the lesson and find myself afloat on that blessing.

One such miracle occurred on August 31, 2017. It was a beautiful summer day. I had just picked fresh vegetables from my garden and was in my kitchen cleaning them. All of my pups were fast asleep. The peace and quiet was soothing. It was the perfect afternoon. Moments later, I heard a quiet thump on the sliding glass door. When I went to the door I looked down to see the most beautiful iridescent moss-green and petal-pink hummingbird lifeless on the ground. I remembered how I had buried one of these little beauties just the previous year, and I felt empowered to change the ending of this bird's story.

I gathered a washcloth and a small shoe box and gently scooped the breathless, delicate, feathered fairy onto the soft cloth. I sat down on a bench in the warm sun with the intention to wish and pray this little one back to life. For thirty minutes I contemplated the power of God when faith is present. Moments of doubt found their way in, telling me that this bird was dead and I would soon bury it just like I had the last. As quickly as these thoughts snuck in, I pushed them out and felt with all my heart that a miracle was about to happen. I spoke with God as I do every morning outside in the break of day. I assured him that I felt his work and the healing of this creature rolling in from the sacred sky above.

I sat in the stillness of the promise and glanced down periodically for a sign of life. Not even a subtle breath could be seen moving through the tiny, still body. But I felt certain that the warm sun was a sovereign remedy and a soothing prescription for renewal. I had to keep the faith that this miracle would indeed unfold.

Thirty-five minutes later, my little friend opened his slender bill as if doing so for the very first time, opening and closing very slowly three times. My senses were heightened. I did my best to contain my astonishment so I wouldn't disrupt or jostle this delicate little blessing. His eyes closed again. I sat still, looking at every beautiful feather, and then his bill opened and closed again three more times. I sat straight up and felt an amazing energy run through my entire body. I held my breath with unbounded hope, and suddenly my feathered friend sat up straight, gracefully pivoted his neck and turned to look at me.

This was happening. I sat before God and Universe, within the ceremony of a miracle. The sweet hummingbird stayed with me, allowing me to melt into the awe of what was happening. After two more tender glances at me, as if to prepare me and say his goodbyes, he took flight. I sat in the glowing sun and whispered praise and gratitude for the gift that was just imparted upon the little bird and me. Both of us were infused with the breath of life.

Later that summer and not long after that beautiful experience, I was outside with the sunrise, watering my garden before the heat of the day set in. The pink sky opened to a fiery orange, and everything outside seemed to awaken at once.

The music of the morning is my favorite of all, ever changing with each new day. The birds always come straight to life at daybreak, and it's not uncommon for me to see our neighborhood fox making his morning rounds, but it's not so typical for the butterflies to greet the early morning. Mid-afternoon seems to be the butterflies' chosen time to dance among the blossoms and the warmer afternoon sun.

But that morning was unique in more ways than one. I had a watering hose in one hand while I fell into the beauty of the morning and slipped into a quick daydream. Something tickled my other hand, and I looked down to see a beautiful butterfly alight on my hand. I kept still, thinking this visit would be brief, but it stayed. I walked to my bench and sat quietly, and so did the butterfly. I was graced with another minute with this normally busy, fluttering creature, and I soaked it all in.

There are gifts in each and every day. Listen to the voice in the silence. It is in the stillness that you will receive your gifts. It is in the stillness that the natural world brings you into its quiet and magnificent beauty brimming with gifts.

CHAPTER 8

A Mantra of Silence

[The American Indian] believes profoundly in silence—the sign of perfect equilibrium. Silence is the absolute poise or balance of body, mind and spirit. If you ask: "What are the fruits of silence?" he will say: "They are self-control, true courage or endurance, patience, dignity, and reverence. Silence is the cornerstone of character."

—Charles Alexander Eastman (Ohiyesa), Santee Sioux

ANCIENT WISDOMS AND MANY religions teach us to repeat words and sounds called "mantras." These positive words encourage peace and calm and connection to a serenity within us. This higher level of thinking renews us and expands our energy and presence with poise, composure and balance. Our thoughts and words are energy moving through us. When this energy is clear and supported with awareness in our words, we experience enlightenment, peace and love.

I have come to believe that our thoughts and words matter in a tremendous way—that they are a cornerstone of our character just as silence is. Silence allows us to gather our thoughts and settle. Positive thoughts garner encouraging, considerate words. Mindful words give us the power to change our lives and the lives of others. There is a beautiful rhythm in the space between silence and words—a measured space where discernment and love are let in.

I spent what I now regard as precious time in the silence. For four years I inquired into my life, my friendships, my role in my family and my future. I looked straight into the mirror and into the reality of who I was. I purged emotions. I uncovered truths and I deliberately studied my own thoughts and words. This reflection brought me directly and honestly to my shortcomings, and I saw just how unaware I was of the impact of my thinking and speaking. The more I committed myself, practiced, and observed the various consequences of my speech and thoughts, the more contemplative I became. Slowing down my thoughts and my responses allowed time for deep consideration that rendered open-hearted purpose and positive intention. I began to feel at peace.

Our words are the end result of the channel of our emotions. They travel through us and fill our thoughts. They resonate in the world and demonstrate who we are. Whether we communicate through speech or the written word, we are communicating a message. We are exposing an expression of ourselves. And whether we are communicating with another or having a conversation in our own minds, it is critical to our well-being and the well-being of others that we mindfully choose what we say.

Words are tremendously powerful. Thoughts are tremendously powerful. We can reset and transform our lives with positive and thoughtful intention in our choices. Change your life by changing your words. Become aware of what you choose to diffuse into the lives of others. Energy that you send out into the world also nestles deep in your spirit and affects the balance of your own energy and your well-being.

Too many words become a distraction. They carry us away from our authentic selves. There are times when the answer is not in the spoken sounds but in the silence. If we comfortably rest in the silence and honorably receive, we stimulate a loving vibration that emanates from within—an acceptance of what is truly before us. We acquire valuable knowledge that would otherwise be wasted in reckless chatter. Sometimes, your truth is told in your silence.

Sit in the silence with these grounding thoughts of Kahlil Gibran:

> You talk when you cease to be at peace with your thoughts; and when you can no longer dwell in the solitude of your heart you live in your lips, and sound is a diversion and a pastime. And in much of your talking, thinking is half murdered. For thought is a bird of space, that in a cage of words may indeed unfold its wings but cannot fly.
>
> There are those among us who seek the talkative for fear of being alone. The silence of aloneness reveals to their eyes their naked selves and they would escape. And there are those who talk, and without knowledge or forethought reveal a truth which they themselves do not understand. And there are those that have the truth within them, but tell it not in words. In the bosom of such as these the spirit dwells in rhythmic silence. When you meet your friend on the roadside or in the market place, let the spirit in you move your lips and direct your tongue. Let the voice within your voice speak to the ear of his ear; for his soul will keep the truth of your heart as the taste of wine is remembered. When the color is forgotten and the vessel is no more.

Before I found the comfort of silence, I too spoke without forethought. I sat constantly determined to fill an awkward space so silence could not seep in. I didn't always understand my talking point, and many times the words would launch out of my mouth before I could claim them as mine.

Truth and transformation can be painful. Purging the thoughts and words that have you stuck can be incredibly uncomfortable because it brings you straight to your own essence. If you feel out of balance in your thoughts and speech, pause and refresh. Change sits you down to honestly examine your behavior. If you are willing to sit with it and be true to yourself, the dishonor soon turns into growth, and the caring, humble, present person that you have always been is uncovered. Spend some time with humility, simply being honest with yourself about your weaknesses.

All of us have weaknesses and flaws. I like to think of flaws as lessons. If we truly strive to refine and enlighten ourselves, these lessons become sacred tools that are necessary for our expansion. As you grow, peace is found in the company of truth. A new stage of development can be welcomed as you come to realize the power in being honest with yourself. Take hold of yourself and know your potential to purify your reaction system and your words. Master the ability to bring your highest presence to the table. Don't allow your first response out. Practice and learn to stop yourself and create your very best response. Set your ego aside and be the student. Patience and intention will create the shift, but remember that as students we don't master each lesson immediately. Simply recognizing our missteps with a vow to do better the next time is walking on the path toward refinement. Yogi Bhajan once said, "Life is a gift too beautiful to be handled by your ego. It can only be handled by your grace."

Oftentimes, we frame people or situations that make us uncomfortable with erroneous assumptions that cause us to utter unnecessary and insensitive words that hurt. The pain isn't just projected onto the other person; it also lodges uneasily in our core and if left unattended can cause disease. Consider the word *dis-ease* as it is spaced out in the dictionary and think about pieces of the definition—disordered or incorrectly functioning system of the body resulting from unfavorable surrounding factors. Release the damaging pressure and tension and circle back to ease and well-being. Being reactive comes from constantly moving without reflection. When we stop, we see that there is something else before us. Surrendering to the truth is where the clarity dwells.

There is so much serenity, space and freedom in the surrender. When we allow hurtful words to reside in our minds and thoughtlessly cross our tongues, the process becomes repetitive and second nature, creating an attachment and holding us hostage in our redundant, low-level thinking. Raising our spirit from negative to positive transforms us from weak to strong. If we make a choice to expand our thoughts and language into a realm that nurtures heart and soul, we experience harmony and an enriching energy that stimulates our being. Learning control allows us to see beyond our perceptions and let go of assumptions, turning the judgement into an acknowledgment of truth, therefore leaving the situation better than it was found.

Carefully chosen words communicating a message with sound intention and honor isn't always our experience. And as much as we intend to improve our presence and connection with others, others might not share our esteem and our same awareness.

If you bump up against an unkind spirit or an abrasive person, think of it as a test for yourself and see the opportunity for growth. Recognize their fears and their place on their own individual journey. See yourself in them. Choose to stand calmly in the face of confrontation. And move through the situation with an open mind and heart, always remembering that we are here to learn from each other and help each other reach our highest potential.

What you focus on expands. It expands throughout your being. You might not take the pain away from the other person, but you are certainly not adding to it. This response could be a turning point in their lives as well as yours. If someone speaks to me from a place of anger or fear, I think to myself, *God is not in your heart right now; let him back in.* These compelling words bring me to a place of peace and carry me beyond what stands before me. We don't have to engage in contention and dispute. Understanding and patience create space for growth, enlightenment and love.

When you lay the groundwork for openness in your heart and soul, and choose your words with understanding and love, there's no room for judgment. As Mother Teresa said, "If you judge people, you have no time to love them." Judgment is a flaw in our moral foundation that weighs us down and creates heaviness in our hearts and souls, bringing forth words that reveal our disconnection. Judgment is ego. Together, this duo of powerful forces causes us to lose our focus and creates separation. We are not meant to be separate. One person is not good and the other bad. Learning to become understanding and open-minded is healing. All of us are here to evolve into our best selves. This evolution isn't without challenges. The challenges are our lessons. I know that I don't want to read the same chapter of my life over and over again without editing the mistakes. We learn and expand by changing the scenarios, hence improving our story.

We hear so much about self-love and self-nurturing. I can't think of a better place to start than with the foundation of being honest with our own selves. If we are genuinely honest with ourselves, we won't see the need to judge others because we will see ourselves in them.

As parents, the greatest gift that we can give to our children is the greatest gift we can give to ourselves: living as purely each day as we did on the day we held our child for the first time. Keeping life sacred is the highest expression of love. If we speak with words of judgment, we risk passing this belief or opinion on to our children. We also risk transferring the stifling habits of judgement and separation. In this transference we weigh our children down with a huge burden to carry and sort through in their lives. I realize that I cannot pave a perfect path for my daughter, but I try my best not to litter her walk with anything worthless.

We are often the principal teacher in our child's life; our impact is penetrating. Looking for the innate perfection in everyone is a distinguished characteristic that can transcend generations with continued growth and mindfulness. See God in every life just as you see him in your life and the life of your child. If you are treated badly by someone, take your response out of the equation. Retreat from the immediate feelings of opposition you might want to grab hold of. Change your habitual response. Stand down from what feels uncomfortable. Stop and give yourself a moment to see what is truly happening. This pause will give way to a shift in your understanding. This simple but profound shift is a beautiful gift. Through wisdom and pausing we step into the shoes of others and peer deep into their being, finding a clearer sense of who we want to be. Respond with honor and grace, and one day the other person and your watchful child might rearrange their reactions in a way that is nurturing to all hearts.

There are times that silence must take the place of words. In the temporary silence, the most honorable words eventually find their way to the surface. Hold a space within yourself for the compassion and healing of those that have hurt you. And then forgive.

Be mindful in forgiving. It is a sacred process. Arriving to a place of true forgiveness takes a willingness to know your own soul and, above all, truly love yourself. When a peaceful light burns deep down inside you, forgiveness becomes the lesson. Forgiveness isn't made up of words; it is made up of love, grace, understanding, and ultimately letting go.

In order to live a life with character and integrity, we must recognize when we see divergence from the truth, and we must refuse to accept it. We know in our hearts what feels right and what doesn't, what seems true and what doesn't, what hurts others and how it feels to be hurt. Have the courage to change the direction and color of a conversation that doesn't serve anyone. We eventually become influenced by the conversations that we choose to engage in, so choose them wisely. Value yourself enough to live the truth in all aspects of your life. Erase judgment, poor perceptions and assumptions from your word choices and your thoughts. Nothing is ever as it seems.

As we make a clear choice to rewrite the story and shift toward understanding our differences, our perceptions align with reality. Each one of us exists at different levels of consciousness, but we exist together. Each of us sees the same things very differently. We are here to move toward greater wisdom. We are here to move amongst one another and hopefully nurture and inspire the light of truth, holding it in our hearts and emitting light and love into our world.

Remember that perceptions have power too. When your perception shifts, your story shifts. Let go of the history of your thoughts. Clear it and hit reset. Use your heart to see others. When you commit to raise your consciousness, you help others to raise theirs. This doesn't mean changing them; it simply means that you are present before them as your most honest self—your best self.

Honesty is the highest form of intimacy and a true gift in forging a humble connection with the souls of others. Be honest with your words and your thoughts. Give yourself this gift of freedom and clarity. It is here in the truth that you will find your peace, your balance, and the place where you rest in unshakable ease. It is in the silence—the space that you give yourself to breathe and to collect your thoughts, the pause that allows you to come back to your heart and the quiet—that softens presumption and leads you back to oneness. Silence is the sound of healing.

LAKOTA INSTRUCTIONS FOR LIVING

"Friend, do it this way—that is, whatever you do in life, do the very best you can with both your heart and mind. And if you do it that way, the Power Of The Universe will come to your assistance, if your heart and mind are in Unity. When one sits in the Hoop Of The People, one must be responsible because All of Creation is related. And the hurt of one is the hurt of all. And the honor of one is the honor of all. And whatever we do affects everything in the Universe. If you do it that way—that is, if you truly join your heart and your mind as One—whatever you ask for, that's the way it's going to be."—*Passed down from White Buffalo Calf Woman*

CHAPTER 9

Grace Is Love in Motion

I VIVIDLY REMEMBER SITTING around our dinner table as a young child, antsy to eat and fill my empty stomach. Toward day's end, I would run down our street as the beckoning gong of our dinner bell brought an end to my afternoon of play. Our dinner bell was mighty. It sat securely atop a twelve-foot wooden pylon just outside our back door. I'm not sure where my dad found our tremendous gathering bell, but I'm sure that every neighbor heard it loud and clear every time he pulled the rope to clang the bell and summon his children home for dinner.

After the nine of us settled around the table, one of us was chosen to say grace. I never really gave thought to the meaning of the word "grace." At the time, it was the only thing that stood between dinner and me. The person that delivered the praise inevitably gave thanks for the food before us. Food was obviously foremost on our minds. As an adult, I don't say grace before my meal unless I'm seated as a guest at someone's table that does, and then, I politely bow my head, curious to hear what others are thankful for, always charmed by the reflection.

I guess a lot of families call this pre-meal blessing "grace." And I'm guessing that there are loads of kids out there that repeat the drill day after day, meal after meal without contemplation of the meaning of this word. I think of how nice the conversation could be, especially in today's world. What is grace?

As an adult, I have realized my interpretation of the meaning of "grace." I have felt it in my soul. I have heard its kindness in my thoughts and its compassion in my words. For me, grace feels like God's warm embrace. Grace is my hope for humanity, my prayer from wherever I stand from this day forward. Mahatma Gandhi said that prayer is "a longing of the soul. It is an admission of one's weakness." My soul longed to discover my weaknesses and transform them into strengths through forgiveness and love. Unearthing my shortcomings gave me the opportunity to transcend my weaknesses as well as those I once saw in others. I now see potential, so much potential in myself and in everyone I love and those I will love in the days to come.

The ethereal hand of the Divine comes to us through the grace of a beautiful breeze, a calming rain, a dreamy sky at dusk, and in so many other simple experiences. Grace is harmony, hope and gratitude. It is a heartfelt, pure and one-on-one conversation with God. Grace is a radiant feeling that can exist in all of us. It is a golden thread that connects us and leads us to our best selves.

The words *conversations with grace* appeared in my mind day after day as I made adjustments toward discovering my life's meaning. I felt the essence of these words, and the strong need to write. After a while, I envisioned a book cover with these very words as the title. The vivid impressions looped through my mind, inspiring my energy to take hold and respond with a plan. The predominant energy pulled me and convinced me not to resist it. I have learned so much from the challenges in my life that brought me to grace. My heart rests open and eager to share that through grace we can not only survive our most difficult intervals of life, we can evolve from them.

In order to feel this pull and hear the still voice inside, I stopped and stood open to the mystery. I connected to the energy, and it carried me along, showing me the importance of reviewing and surveying my life up to that point. In order to feel a harmonious flow of tranquility in my life, I needed to shed my basic ideas and learn to understand and embrace the very essence of connectedness.

This would require diligence and an open mind. An open mind also meant a clean mind without the distraction of my ego. Until we move our egos out of the way, our intuition is muted, and we move about unaware of our greatest potential. Our egos construct walls that impede our growth and block our meaningful acceptance of oneness.

We build obstacles in our lives by not paying attention to our intuition and not heeding the divine, graceful voice that tries to lead us to where we belong. I knew in my bones that this new road that I chose to walk would significantly affect the ones I loved, especially my daughter.

I wanted her life to be different than mine. Our lives have their own natural course, but I believe that I am an integral part of her course. I took my influence on her life very seriously. I chose to elevate my thinking, speaking and awareness. I chose to exemplify an awakened life for her. I was cognizant of how my growth would render a better life for my daughter, my husband and everyone that I share my heart with.

My intention on this day and in my days ahead is not to leave barriers in her path but to adorn her passage through life with love, grace and virtue. I chose to settle in and create space in my life for new beginnings.

At the midpoint in my life, I found the door to my soul and I opened it. The pull was magnetic. The natural world revealed the silence and grace essential for me to perceive the Divine in the purest sense, and in this enchanting refuge, I found the answers. I knew that I needed to follow an alternate path that would lead me back to my life.

I continue to feel the rousing energy of a divine spirit guiding me to stay the course. This extraordinary energy, sourced from grace, has filled me with profound peace and delight in knowing that I am just fine in the company of myself. I am better now for what I thought was loneliness. I am better now for the stillness that expands my mind into a direct connection to the magical love of the Divine. It is within this connection that I have experienced remarkable miracles in my life. This penetrating and intense sense of oneness is now nestled deep within me, and it carries a power that is so expansive and true that I can feel it radiate into the hearts of others.

I continue to inquire everyday into my energy and grace. I ask myself, *Am I living harmlessly? Am I holding and sharing pure love? Am I seeing with the eyes of my soul and seeing the Divine in everyone?* These are questions that I will continue to ask myself until my heart and soul know no other way.

The soul is full of wisdom and patience, and our soul's intention is always just within us. When the mind is calm, the soul is able to guide. Intuition is a pure sense of our soul, full of brilliance and divination. Alignment with our intuition occurs when we listen to our true feelings. As the Native American proverb reminds us, "Our first teacher is our own heart."

We must get out of our minds and into our hearts. Our heart is the center of our emotions and a more powerful gauge than our brain. If we soften the energies in our emotions, we soften our hearts and allow ourselves to hear the voice of silence. It is in this peace that the essence of source and grace flow effortlessly.

Give yourself the gift of being alone. Find the silence and connect to nature. Feel your soul. Kindle your graceful light. Feel the love that exists in your heart for everyone, especially yourself. Allow the energy and vibrations to come to you through your heart. Connect to it. Allow the Divine voice to be heard. Let your spirit speak to you. The heart lets us know when we are forcing something and when we are in alignment. Embrace and strengthen your internal connection to natural, comfortable feelings. As serenity spans your being, feel your mind empty of unnecessary clutter and simply trust. Go within and stay there. Get comfortable and observe as you emerge into your connected self, primed to soar to your highest level while radiating a forgiving and loving light. The more steeped you become in the silence, the more aware you become. The Divine guides each one of us, as we are ready.

The more I stripped myself down, the more potent my life became. My connection to nature became more potent. My connection to God became more potent. The silence became more potent. The uncomfortable became comfortable. I grew into my soul by honoring everything and coming to stand in the integrity of the present moment. I withstood every powerful storm in my life and now felt the power of perpetual grace. I felt grace in my humility and in my courage. I felt it in my forgiveness and understanding. And I felt it deeply in my connection to God and the power of love.

I will never forget the comforting vision and sweet sound of a family friend singing "Amazing Grace" at the graveside of my mother-in-law, Jodie. "Amazing Grace" was Jodie's favorite song. She would have been so proud of the beautiful melody surrounding her place of rest. The words "I once was lost but now am found" simply floated through the air back then, but today the words clearly resonate with me, boldly summing up my own life. Mind you, I'm not the girl sitting in the church pew these days, but I am outside in the amazing grace of nature where I have experienced miracles that are filled with profound healing and a love that is grace. My temple is my body, heart and mind.

Grace is finding a different language to speak to yourself and to others no matter your situation. It's about changing the conversation in your head and in your heart and rising above the separation and into the grace that exists within all of us.

As much as we sometimes believe that we are a bundle of fear or regret, we are also a bundle of possibility. Step into the understanding that waits in the love that you seek and the love that has been within you all along. The most beautiful revelation is when you feel for the first time that this is where you're supposed to be.

Challenge yourself to feel the pull and remember why you are here. Be honest, be kind to yourself and others, manifest grace in every aspect of your life and remember the wisdom of Khalil Gibran: "Your daily life is your temple and your religion." Let the grace you speak not only be spoken before a meal, but also with every word. Shine the light on your goodness, and honor what is worthy. Be as windows flung wide open—giving and receiving a beautiful flow of fresh, clean energy that travels across the earth, affecting every life with love and grace.

There is a sky full of stars and a luminous moon above our heads every night just waiting for us to make wishes upon and take in the vast calm. Our earth turns on its axis, and the seasons change along some remarkable intrinsic schedule, keeping us moving forward. The sun rises at the break of every morning, softening our hearts and slowing our breath. As these extraordinary blessings are showered upon all of us each and every day, we are given another chance to awaken our consciousness. We are given the golden opportunity every morning to live in reciprocity, to live in the extraordinary goodness that is so lovingly and freely bestowed upon us with the grace of the natural world. As Mark Twain once said, "The two most important days in your life are the day you were born and the day you find out why."

For your heart and mine, I pray this tender Tibetan blessing: "May you be filled with loving kindness. May you be well. May you be peaceful and at ease. May you be happy."

Acknowledgments

For the children and young adults in my life,
I thank you for making me better.

Go and see new places, learn, meet new friends, understand people everywhere better; hear them, listen to their stories, look into their eyes, tell them who you are, change together into a life without perception, assumptions and judgement, and then come back to the table with your stories of love. This is my wish.

BOOK CLUB DISCUSSION QUESTIONS

1. Silence can sometimes make us feel uncomfortable and eager to fill the void, but allowing it can be both calming and informative. In the calm, we are able to hear the voice of our intuition as the truth rises to the surface. Are you comfortable in silence? What does silence sound like to you?

2. If you have a relationship or two in your life that present challenges or anxiety, would you consider and possibly commit to changing your thinking about the person and the role that you have played?

3. Stress never feels as natural as peace. Why do you think that we sometimes choose stress over peace?

4. It has been said that death is a part of life, not the opposite of life. Death is heartbreaking, and navigating through the grief can be excruciating. Have you ever worked through the death of a loved one to a place where you now feel settled knowing that death is indeed a part of life?

5. When faced with adversity, are you more apt to turn inward or away from the pain, or do you see yourself honestly and truthfully with a willingness to grow?

6. How would you define love?

7. Have you ever considered spending time inquiring into your own habits and thoughts, meeting them with clarity and understanding? Do you feel that you could benefit and transform your life by calling forth what is in you?

8. Do you believe that everyone and everything on this earth is connected? Do you feel a connection to life around you? Do you feel the vast difference between connectedness and separation?

9. Have you ever considered spending your day focused on and holding a feeling of love for yourself and everyone you cross paths with? When I say everyone, I especially mean those people in your life that present you with challenge.

10. What are your gifts that you can share with the world? Are you sharing them? If not, what holds you back?